THE LANGUAGE
OF OPPRESSION

Haig A. Bosmajian
University of Washington

PUBLIC AFFAIRS PRESS, WASHINGTON, D. C.

The language of oppression has been of special concern to Haig Bosmajian (Ph.D., Stanford University) ever since the late 1950's when he began his research into the techniques of Nazi persuasion.

Some of Dr. Bosmajian's recent articles—notably "The Language of White Racism" *(College English)*, "Speech and the First Amendment" *(Today's Speech)*, and "The Language of Sexism" ETC.—have attracted considerable attention and have been widely reprinted. Adaptations of several of the articles appear in these pages by special permission.

Among the books edited or co-edited by the author are *The Principles and Practice of Freedom of Speech* (1971), *Dissent: Symbolic Behavior and Rhetorical Strategies* (1972), *This Great Argument: The Rights of Women* (1972), *The Rhetoric of the Civil Rights Movement* (1969), and *Obscenity and Freedom of Expression* (1974).

CONTENTS

1

INTRODUCTION

"Sticks and stones may break my bones, but words can never hurt me." To accept this adage as valid is sheer folly. "What's in a name? that which we call a rose by any other name would smell as sweet." The answer to Juliet's question is "Plenty!" and to her own response to the question we can only say that this is by no means invariably true. The importance, significance, and ramifications of naming and defining people cannot be over-emphasized. From *Genesis* and beyond, to the present time, the power which comes from naming and defining people has had positive as well as negative effects on entire populations.

The magic of words and names has always been an integral part of both "primitive" and "civilized" societies. As Margaret Schlauch has observed, "from time immemorial men have thought there is some mysterious essential connection between a thing and the spoken name for it. You could use the name of your enemy, not only to designate him either passionately or dispassionately, but also to exercise a baleful influence." [1]

Biblical passages abound in which names and naming are endowed with great power; from the very outset, in *Genesis,* naming and defining are attributed a significant potency: "And out of the ground the Lord God formed every beast of the field and every fowl of the air; and brought them unto Adam to see what he would call them: and whatsoever Adam called every living creature, that was the name thereof." [2] Amidst the admonitions in *Leviticus* against theft, lying, and fraud is the warning: "And ye shall not swear my

1

name falsely, neither shalt thou profane the name of thy God: I am the Lord." [3] So important is the name that it must not be blasphemed; those who curse and blaspheme shall be stoned "and he that blasphemeth the name of the Lord, he shall surely be put to death, and all the congregation shall certainly stone him." [4] So important is the name that the denial of it is considered a form of punishment: "But ye are they that foresake the Lord, that forget my holy mountain. . . . Therefore will I number you to the sword, and ye shall all bow down to the slaughter: because when I called, ye did not answer; when I spake, ye did not hear. . . . Therefore thus saith the Lord God, behold, my servants shall eat, but ye shall be hungry. . . . And ye shall leave your name for a curse unto my chosen: for the Lord God shall slay thee, and call his servants by another name." [5]

To be unnamed is to be unknown, to have no identity. William Saroyan has observed that "the word nameless, especially in poetry and in much prose, signifies an alien, unknown, and almost unwelcome condition, as when, for instance, a writer speaks of 'a nameless sorrow.'" "Human beings," continues Saroyan, "are for the fact of being named at all, however meaninglessly, lifted out of an area of mystery, doubt, or undesirability into an area in which belonging to everybody else is taken for granted, so that one of the first questions asked by new people, two-year-olds even, whether they are speaking to other new people or to people who have been around for a great many years, is 'What is your name?'" [6]

To receive a name is to be elevated to the status of a human being; without a name one's identity is questionable. In stressing the importance of a name and the significance of having none, Joyce Hertzler has said that "among both primitives and moderns, an individual has no definition, no validity for himself, without a name. His name is his badge of individuality, the means whereby he identifies himself and enters upon a truly subjective existence. My own name, for example, stands for me, a person. Divesting me of it reduces me to a meaningless, even pathological, nonentity." [7]

In his book *What Is In A Name?* Farhang Zabeeth reminds us that "the Roman slaves originally were without names. Only after being sold they took their master's praenomen in the genitive case followed by the suffix — 'por' (boy), e.g., 'Marcipor,' which indicates that some men, so long as they were regarded by others as cattle, did not need a name. However, as soon as they became servants some designation was called forth." [8] To this day one of the forms of punishment meted out to wrongdoers who are imprisoned is to take away their names and to give them numbers. In an increasingly computerized age people are becoming mere numbers—credit card numbers, insurance numbers, bank account numbers, student numbers, et cetera. Identification of human beings by numbers is a negation of their humanity and their existence.

Philologist Max Muller has pointed out that "if we examine the most ancient word for 'name,' we find it is *naman* in Sanskrit, *nomen* in Latin, *namo* in Gothic. This *naman* stands for gnaman and is derived from the root, *gna*, to know, and meant originally that by which we know a thing." [9] In the course of the evolution of human society, R. P. Masani tells us, the early need for names "appears to have been felt almost simultaneously with the origin of speech . . . personality and the rights and obligations connected with it would not exist without the name." [10] In his classic work *The Golden Bough* James Frazer devotes several pages to tabooed names and words in ancient societies, taboos reflecting the power and magic people saw in names and words. Frazer notes, for example, that "the North American Indian 'regards his name, not as a mere label, but as a distinct part of his personality, just as much as are his eyes or his teeth, and believes that injury will result as surely from the malicious handling of his name as from a wound inflicted on any part of his physical organism." [11]

A name can be used as a curse. A name can be blasphemed. Name-calling is so serious a matter that statutes and court decisions prohibit "fighting words" to be uttered. In 1942 the United States Supreme Court upheld the conviction of a person who had addressed a police officer as "a God damned racketeer" and "a damned Fascist." (*Chaplinsky v. New Hampshire*, 315 U. S. 568). Such namecalling, such epithets, said the Court, are not protected speech. So important is one's "good name" that the law prohibits libel.

History abounds with instances in which the mere utterance of a name was prohibited. In ancient Greece, according to Frazer, "the names of the priests and other high officials who had to do with the performance of the Eleusinian mysteries might not be uttered in their lifetime. To pronounce them was a legal offense." [12] Jorgen Ruud reports in *Taboo: A Study of Malagasy Customs and Beliefs* that among the Antandroy people the father has absolute authority in his household and that "children are forbidden to mention the name of their father. They must call him father, daddy. . . . The children may not mention his house or the parts of his body by their ordinary names, but must use other terms, i.e., euphemisms." [13]

It was Iago who said in *Othello:*

> *Who steals my purse steals trash; 'tis some-*
> > *thing nothing;*
> *'Twas mine, 'tis his, and has been slave to*
> > *thousands;*

But he that filches from me my good name
Robs me of that which not enriches him
And makes me poor indeed.

Alice, in Lewis Carroll's *Through the Looking Glass*, had trepidations about entering the woods where things were nameless: "This must be the wood," she said thoughtfully to herself, "where things have no names. I wonder what'll become of *my* name when I go in? I shouldn't like to lose it at all—because they'd have to give me another, and it would almost certain to be an ugly one."

A Nazi decree of August 17, 1938 stipulated that "Jews may receive only those first names which are listed in the directives of the Ministry of the Interior concerning the use of first names." Further, the decree provided: "If Jews should bear first names other than those permitted...they must ... adopt an additional name. For males, that name shall be Israel, for females Sara." Another Nazi decree forbade Jews in Germany "to show themselves in public without a Jew's star. . . . [consisting] of a six-pointed star of yellow cloth with black borders, equivalent in size to the palm of the hand. The inscription is to read 'JEW' in black letters. It is to be sewn to the left breast of the garment, and to be worn visibly."

The power which comes from names and naming is related directly to the power to define others—individuals, races, sexes, ethnic groups. Our identities, who and what we are, how others see us, are greatly affected by the names we are called and the words with which we are labelled. The names, labels, and phrases employed to "identify" a people may in the end determine their survival. The word "define" comes from the Latin *definire*, meaning to limit. Through definition we restrict, we set boundaries, we name.

"When I use a word," said Humpty Dumpty in *Through*

the Looking Glass, "it means just what I choose it to mean—neither more nor less." "The question is," said Alice, "whether you can make words mean so many different things." "The question is," said Humpty Dumpty, "which is to be master—that's all."

During his days as a civil rights-black power activist, Stokely Carmichael accurately asserted: "It [definition] is very, very important because I believe that people who can define are masters." [14] Self-determination must include self-definition, the ability and right to name oneself; the master-subject relationship is based partly on the master's power to name and define the subject.

While names, words and language can be and are used to inspire us, to motivate us to humane acts, to liberate us, they can also be used to dehumanize human beings and to "justify" their suppression and even their extermination. It is not a great step from the coercive suppression of dissent to the extermination of dissenters (as the United States Supreme Court declared in its 1943 compulsory flag salute opinion in *West Virginia State Board of Education v. Barnette*); nor is it a large step from defining a people as non-human or sub-human to their subjugation or annihilation. One of the first acts of an oppressor is to redefine the "enemy" so they will be looked upon as creatures warranting separation, suppression, and even eradication.

The Nazis redefined Jews as "bacilli," "parasites," "disease," "demon," and "plague." In his essay "The Hollow Miracle," George Steiner informs us that the Germans "who poured quicklime down the openings of the sewers in Warsaw to kill the living and stifle the stink of the dead wrote about it. They spoke of having to 'liquidate vermin'. . . . Gradually, words lost their original meaning and acquired nightmarish definitions. *Jude, Pole, Russe* came to mean two-legged lice, putrid vermin which good Aryans must squash, as a [Nazi] Party manual said, 'like roaches on a dirty wall.' 'Final solution,' *endgültige Lösung*, came to signify the death of six million human beings in gas ovens." [15]

The language of white racism has for centuries been used to "keep the nigger in his place." Our sexist language has allowed men to define who and what a woman is and must be. Labels like "traitors," "saboteurs," "queers," and "obscene degenerates" were applied indiscriminately to students who protested the war in Vietnam or denounced injustices in the United States. Are such people to be listened to? Consulted? Argued with? Obviously not! One does not listen to, much less talk to, traitors and outlaws, sensualists and queers. One only punishes them or, as Spiro Agnew suggested in one of his 1970 speeches, there are some dissenters who should be separated "from our society with no more regret than we should feel over discarding rotten apples." [16]

What does it mean to separate people? When the Japanese-Americans were rounded up in 1942 and sent off to "relocation camps" they were "separated." The Jews in Nazi Germany were "separated." The Indians of the United States, the occupants of the New World before Columbus "discovered" it, have been systematically "separated." As "chattels" and slaves, the blacks in the United States were "separated"; legally a black person was a piece of property, although human enough to be counted as three-fifths of a person in computing the number of people represented by white legislators.

How is the forcible isolation of human beings from society at large justified? To make the separation process more palatable to the populace, what must the oppressor first do? How does he make the populace accept the separation of the "creatures," or, if not accept it, at least not protest it? Consideration of such questions is not an academic exercise without practical implications. There is a close nexus between language and self-perception, self-awareness, self-identity, and self-esteem. Just as our thoughts affect our language, so does our language affect our thoughts and eventually our actions and behavior. As Edward Sapir has observed, we are all "at the mercy of the particular language which has become the medium of expression" in our society. The "real world," he points out, "is to a large extent unconsciously built up on the language habits of the group.... We see and hear and otherwise experience very largely as we do because the language habits of our community predispose certain choices of interpretation." [17]

George Orwell has written in his famous essay "Politics and the English Language": "A man may take to drink because he feels himself to be a failure, and then fail all the more completely because he drinks. It is rather the same thing that is happening to the English language. It becomes ugly and inaccurate because our thoughts are foolish, but the slovenliness of our language makes it easier for us to have foolish thoughts." [18] Orwell maintains that "the decadence in our language is probably curable" and that "silly words and expressions have often disappeared, not through any evolutionary process but owing to the conscious action of a minority." [19] Wilma Scott Heide, speaking as president of the National Organization for Women several years ago, indicated that feminists were undertaking this conscious action: "In any social movement, when changes are effected, the language sooner or later reflects the change. Our approach is different. Instead of passively noting the change, we are changing language patterns to actively effect the changes, a significant part of which is the conceptual tool of thought, our language." [20]

This then is our task — to identify the decadence in our language, the inhumane uses of language, the "silly words and expressions" which have been used to justify the unjustifiable, to make palatable the unpalatable, to make reasonable the unreasonable, to make decent the indecent. Hitler's "Final Solution" appeared reasonable once the Jews were successfully labelled by the Nazis as sub-humans, as "parasites," "vermin," and "bacilli." The segregation and suppression of blacks in the United States was justified once they were considered "chattels" and "inferiors." The subjugation of the "American Indians" was defensible since they were defined as "barbarians" and "savages." As Peter Farb has said, "cannibalism, torture, scalping, mutilation, adultery, incest, sodomy, rape, filth, drunkenness — such a catalogue of accusations against a people is an indication not so much of their depravity as that their land is up for grabs." [21] As long as adult women are "chicks," "girls," "dolls," "babes," and "ladies," their status in society will remain "inferior"; they will go on being treated as subjects in the subject-master relationship as long as the language of the law places them into the same class as children, minors, and the insane.

It is my hope that an examination of the language of oppression will result in a conscious effort by the reader to help cure this decadence in our language, especially that language which leads to dehumanization of the human being. One way for us to curtail the use of the language of oppression is for those who find themselves being defined into subjugation to rebel against such linguistic suppression. It isn't strange that those persons who insist on defining themselves, who insist on this elemental privilege of self-naming, self-definition, and self-identity encounter vigorous resistance. Predictably, the resistance usually comes from the oppressor or would-be oppressor and is a result of the fact that he or she does not want to relinquish the power which comes from the ability to define others.

2

THE LANGUAGE OF ANTI-SEMITISM

In 1923 Adolf Hitler attempted to take over the German government by an armed march of Nazis on Munich. His *putsch* failed and he was sent to prison for several months, during which he began to write *Mein Kampf*. Ten years later he attained power through an election in which the Nazis amassed 43.9 percent of Germany's votes, enough to secure power with the support of the Nationalists and the illegal exclusion from the Reichstag of 88 legally elected Communist Deputies. During the ten year period 1923-1933 Hitler transformed an insignificant party into Germany's largest single party.

Hitler's successful rise can be partly explained in terms of the societal conditions in Germany, but it was his use of propaganda which in the end got him the support of the German people. The democratic Weimar government, established by the World War I victors, was unable to solve the problems faced by the nation; the victors would not let the people forget the humiliation of losing the war; countless Germans were barely able to feed themselves. Not only had their nation been defeated in war, it was plagued with internal unrest, inflation, and then depression. What Hitler did was promise the humiliated that they once again could be proud Germans; he gave them a scapegoat upon which to vent their frustrations. While the scapegoat was "das System" in general, Hitler pointed to specific individuals and groups upon whom the ills of Germany could be placed. "Men and women," George Mosse tells us in his book *Nazi Culture*, "fell into the arms of the new Reich like ripe fruit from a tree. ... For millions the Nazi ideology did assuage their anxiety, did end their alienation, and did give hope for a better future. Other millions watched passively, not deeply committed to resistance. 'Let them have a chance' was a typical attitude. Hitler took the chance and made the most of it." [1]

Hitler's rise to power can be comprehended more easily if one is aware of the conditions under which charlatanism has thrived. What Grete de Francesco has said in *The Power of the Charlatan,* a study of the seventeenth and eighteenth century shamans and mountebanks in Europe whose potions, salves, and secret remedies were a promise to cure the ills and ailments of the populace, applies in many ways to conditions in Germany between 1920 and 1933 and to Hitler's highly effective techniques of persuasion. Charlatans have thrived under conditions where instability, insecurity, upheaval, and malaise prevailed.

Concerning the mountebanks of the seventeenth and eighteenth centuries, de Francesco said:

"The people flocked around these false prophets ... because they, too, had been disturbed in their religious convictions; the religious wars in the seventeenth century, following the upheaval of the Reformation, had profoundly shaken the spiritual security of Europe. Scourged by plague as well as war, often driven from hearth and home, the people could no longer pursue old patterns of life; the breakdown of established habits brought a new liability in both ideas and emotions. ...

"In times of need, when men must bear heavy burdens of suffering not caused by obvious faults of their own and therefore incomprehensible to them, they tend to herd together around any leader who promises crumbs of comfort." [2]

While exploiting the instability, frustrations, and malaise

of the German people, Hitler did not seriously propose specific rational programs for alleviating the specific economic and political troubles facing Germany. As Leo Lowenthal and Norbert Guterman have observed in their *Prophets of Deceit,* "the agitator does not fit into the reformer type; his grievances are not circumscribed, but on the contrary take in every area of social life. Nor does he address himself to any distinct social group, as does the reformer." [3] Neither does the agitator, say Lowenthal and Guterman, fall into the revolutionary group; the agitator "refers vaguely to the inadequacies and inequities of the existing social structure, but he does not hold it ultimately responsible for social ills, as does the revolutionary." Further: "He always suggests that what is necessary is the elimination of people rather than a change in political structure. Whatever political changes may be involved in the process of getting rid of the enemy he sees as a means rather than an end. The enemy is represented as acting, so to speak, directly on his victims without the intermediary of a social form, such as capitalism is defined to be in socialist theory. For instance, although agitational literature contains frequent references to unemployment, one cannot find in it a discussion of the economic causes of unemployment. The agitator lays responsibility on an unvarying set of enemies, whose evil character or sheer malice is at the bottom of social maladjustment." [4]

As an agitator and charlatan, Adolf Hitler created a phantasmagoria where there simply was no place for discussion or debate regarding the social and political issues confronting the German people. The verbal and nonverbal means of persuasion — including the flags, marching, heroes, music, monuments, mass meetings, goose-stepping parades, fire, blood, eagles, and the scores of other symbols, accompanied by beatings and killings — psychologically pounded millions of Germans into accepting Hitlerism; yet still other millions of Germans who were fascinated with and attracted to the atavistic persuasive appeals willingly and enthusiastically succumbed to the Nazi persuasion, making it possible for Hitler to attain power. On March 5, 1933, in Germany's last free election until after World War II, 39,-655,764 voters went to the polls to give the Nazis 17,277,180 votes which enabled them to seat 288 of their deputies in the Reichstag.

Hitler's choice of propaganda tactics depended chiefly on his estimate of his audiences. The masses, he said, were sentimental, respectful of force, intellectually disinterested, desirous of simplicity, susceptible to emotional contagion, moved by exaggeration, impressed less by knowledge than by fanaticism, and influenced to action not through the mind but through the heart. He said of the German people that their receptivity was very limited, their intelligence small, and their forgetfulness enormous. "What luck," he declared, "for governments that the peoples they administer don't think!" [5]

The masses, Hitler wrote in *Mein Kampf*, are inspired and dominated by fanaticism and sometimes hysteria; they "are only a piece of Nature and their sentiment does not understand the mutual handshake of people who claim that they want opposite things. What they desire is the victory of the stronger and the destruction of the weak and his unconditional subjection." [6] These characteristics he attributed to his German audiences are also the characteristics of the "crowd" and the "crowd mentality" as described by Sigmund Freud in his *Group Psychology:*

"It might be said that the intense emotional ties which we observe in groups [crowds] are quite sufficient to explain one of their characteristics — the lack of independence and initiative in their members, the similarity in the reactions of all of them, their reduction, so to speak, to the level of group individuals. But if we look at it as a whole, a group shows us more than this. Some of its features — weaknesses of intellectual ability, the lack of emotional restraint, the incapacity for moderation and delay, the inclination to exceed every limit in the expression of emotion and to work it off completely in the form of action — these and similar features, which we find so impressively described by LeBon, show an unmistakable picture of a regression of mental activity to an earlier stage such as we are not surprised to find among savages or children." [7]

Since German audiences, as viewed by the Nazis, were irrational, primitive, and feminine in nature, the persuasive devices turned on them were manipulated accordingly. In the case of those Germans who did not possess these characteristics every effort was made to place them in crowd situations where they would lose their individuality, their rational and intellectual qualities. Since the crowd mentality can be sustained more easily when the populace is gripped by fear and insecurity, Hitler capitalized on the perpetual crisis. A secure, individualistic citizenry was of no use to him. As George Devereaux has explained: "Having risen to power through a crisis . . . the dictator automatically seeks to perpetuate the crisis." [8] Instead of allaying fear, the Nazis aroused it; instead of subduing indignation, they encouraged it; instead of diminishing hate, they excited it. All of these emotions were indispensable to Nazi persuasion. Hitler created the crowd mentality and led the people into a state of illusion.

Although the Nazis relied on terror, violence, and intimidation to gain power, they realized that such tactics alone would not carry them to supremacy over the German nation. After his abortive Munich *putsch,* Hitler decided that instead of "working to achieve power by an armed coup, we shall have to hold our noses and enter the Reichstag against the Catholic and Marxist deputies. . . . Sooner or later we shall have a majority — and after that Germany." [9] Physical violence had its place, said Nazi propagandist Eugen Hadamovsky, but propaganda could be more effective than force as a means of persuasion.[10] From the outset in Hitlerism, the propaganda section of the Nazi Party was of central importance. "Hitler's genius as a politician," Alan Bullock says in his biography of *der Fuhrer,* "lay in his unequalled grasp of what could be done by propaganda, and his flair for seeing how to do it." [11]

"I know," Hitler wrote in *Mein Kampf* "that men are won over less by the written word than by the spoken word, that every great movement on this earth owes its growth to great orators and not to great writers." [12]   Dr. Joseph Goebbels stressed the idea of the superiority of the spoken word over the written word in moving the masses. Did Christ, he asked, write books or did he preach? Did Mohammed write intellectual essays or did he go to the people and tell them what he wanted? When Lenin came from Zurich to Petersburg, did he go from the station to the study and write a book or did he not instead speak before thousands? One can prove through history, Goebbels declared, "that the great politician was also a great speaker: Napoleon, Caesar, Alexander, Mussolini, Lenin, you can name whom you want." [13]

Hitler hypothesized in *Mein Kampf* that the French Revolution would never have come about through philosophical theories if it had not been for the "army of agitators led by demagogues in the grand style, who whipped up the passions of the people tormented to begin with, until at last there occurred that terrible volcanic eruption which held all Europe rigid with fear." [14]

The Nazis preferred the spoken to the written word because, for example, an author cannot control the circumstances under which his book is read or not read; the public speaker, on the other hand, can adjust his speech to the situation and if he sees that his audience is losing interest he can do or say something to get back their attention. Reading we do alone; public speaking involves an audience and, according to the Nazis, the emotional contagion which is possible at a mass rally is not possible when one is reading a book or a newspaper. The reader is in a better position to be critical of the material he is reading since he can examine more carefully what is on the written page; the critical abilities of the listener are hampered by the fact that he cannot compel a speaker to provide an explanation. The pen, said Hitler, may provide the theoretical foundations of a movement, but the "power which has always started the greatest religious and political avalanches in history rolling has from time immemorial been the magic power of the spoken word, and that alone." [15]

In a propaganda glutted with ritual, ceremony, flags, blood, fire, banners, heroes, slogans, posters, music, parades, and a constant display of power, there simply was no place for the rational, meaningful use of language. Philosopher Ernst Cassirer has observed that one of the first things Hitler had to do if the Nazi persuasion was to succeed was to bring about a change in the function of language. Cassirer distinguishes between the semantical and the magical uses of words. The magic word, Cassirer reminds us, "does not describe things or relations of things; it tries to produce effects and to change the course of nature. This cannot be done without an elaborate magical art. The magician, or the sorcerer, is alone able to govern the magic word. But in his hands it becomes a most powerful weapon. Nothing can resist its force. '*Carmina vel coelo possunt deducere lunam,*' says the sorceress Medea in Ovid's *Metamorphoses* — by magic songs and incantations even the moon can be dragged down from the heavens." [16]

In dissecting Nazi manipulation of language, Heinz Paechter observed: "Most people think as they talk. 'Man lebt in seiner Sprache,' says Hanns Johst, a pioneer Nazi poet. The language that is spoken in totalitarian countries conveys the climate of the totalitarian mind. It is more than a vehicle of command which helps shape the pattern of a social structure into its ritual." [17] Nazi propagandist Hadamovsky asserted that the "refined old language of diplomacy had to make way for the new, powerful specialized language of political mass propaganda.... Freedom, Equality, Brotherhood, Capitalism, Socialism, Communism, Profit, World Economy, Soviet Deutschland, Nationalism, Blood, Soil, Race, Autocracy, Third Reich—these are some of the *Schlagworte* which connote doctrines and ideologies." [18] Literally translated, *Schlagworte* means "hitting words"; *Schlagen* means "to beat." *Schlagworte* were words which would dull the listener's critical abilities since the listener was "hit" or "struck" with them. "Hitler has much knowledge about the magic of words," a Nazi declared. "The word of a passionate man becomes a weapon. Hitler achieved in a few months more with his words than did the 'statesmen' with their 'deeds' " [19] The Nazis used words, as Grunberger points out in his *A Social History of the Third Reich*, "not as bridges extended to the listener's mind, but as harpoons to be embedded in the soft flesh of their subconscious. The varied usages of speech — as communication, argument,

plaidoyer, monologue, prayer or incantation — were reduced
to one single incantatory one." [20]

The Nazis' perception of their German audiences as
"crowds" possessed by the "crowd mentality" led to a persuasion in which the magic word superseded any rational
approach to the use of language. The crowd, Freud observed,
is subject to the truly magical power of words. He quotes
Gustav LeBon: "Reason and arguments are incapable of
combatting certain words and formulas. They are uttered
with solemnity in the presence of groups, and as soon as they
have been pronounced an expression of respect is visible on
every countenance, all heads are bowed. By many they are
considered as natural forces or as supernatural powers." [21]
Freud added: "It is only necessary in this connection to
remember the taboo upon names and words." It is within the
power of the magician, who has as his audience listeners
possessed of the "crowd mentality," to conjure up words and
cliches which referentially are meaningless, and endow them
with magical power.[22]

Since dialogue and debate as they are known in democratic parliamentary systems existed neither at Nazi meetings
during the *Kampfzeit* (period of struggle, i.e., up to 1933)
nor in the Third Reich, the ambiguity and meaninglessness
of Nazi magic words remained unchallenged. Hitler could
therefore say to his German audiences: "Bear in mind the
devastation which Jewish bastardization visits on our nation
each day, and consider that this blood-poisoning can be removed from our national body only after centuries, if at all;
consider further how racial disintegration drags down and
often destroys the last Aryan values of our German people, so
that our strength as a culture-bearing nation is visibly more
and more involved in a regression and we run the risk, in
our big cities at least, of reaching the point where southern

Italy is today. This contamination of our people is carried on systematically by the Jew today. Systematically these black parasites of the nation defile our inexperienced young blonde girls and thereby destroy something which can no longer be replaced in this world." [23]

"Jewish bastardization." "Blood poisoning." "Racial disintegration." "Contamination of our people." "Black parasites." "Inexperienced blonde girls." What is Aryan blood? How does "non-Aryan blood" poison "Aryan blood?" English writer John Wilson has stated: "An intelligent supporter of Hitler would probably have said: 'When we speak of Aryan blood, you must not understand us too literally. We do not mean that the actual blood of Ayrans is anything special. All that we mean is that Aryans are superior to non-Aryans.' Undoubtedly many Germans appreciated this point, but their leaders continued to use the phrase 'Aryan blood' because it had considerable emotional appeal for their followers. 'Blood' is a word which we tend to invest with magical force." [24] It isn't difficult to understand how so many Germans succumbed to this appeal, says Wilson, "when we remember how seriously we used to take the so-called blue blood of our own [British] aristocracy, and how most people did indeed think that there was something actually in the blood of kings and nobles which was substantially different from the blood of commoners." [25]

The Nazis purposely used terminology which appeared concrete but was in reality ambiguous and meaningless. The "enemies" of Germany that had to be destroyed and eliminated, said Hitler, were the "Red Dragon," the "Jewish bacillus," the "democratic-Marxist-Jew," the "parliamentarians," and the "November criminals," the latter including anyone associated with the establishment of the Weimar Republic after World War I. All these abstractions were in turn grouped together into an equally abstract "das System." Nazi propagandist Franz Six explained the need for creation of "das System": "If too many opponents are shown to one's own members, then the danger is that the inner solidarity and unity is corrupted by the feeling of inferiority which arises. Therefore, it is the task of a logically conducted propaganda to unite the opponents—even if they possess different characteristics and strive towards different goals — under one concept and to direct the strength of the attack against them as a whole.... 'Das System' became the great point of attack, the object against which National Socialist agitation could drive the masses through the simplest and most easily understood formulas. It did not matter if this concept of 'das System' meant the Republic, the Marxist, or the Liberal government. In any case, it had become necessary to create a popular slogan in the battle against present conditions which could incite and reach, through its brutality, the hate of the unemployed worker as well as the farmer aching under taxation. [The term 'das System'] should unveil a spiritual emptiness of a state which had become, in its outer form as well as in its inner constitution, similar to the mechanism of a machine." [26]

Herr Six was merely repeating what Hitler had emphasized in *Mein Kampf:* "It belongs to the genius of a great leader to make even adversaries far removed from one another seem to belong to a single category, because in weak and uncertain characters the knowledge of having different enemies can only too readily lead to the beginning of doubt in their own right. Once the wavering mass sees itself in a struggle against too many enemies, objectivity will put in an appearance, throwing open the question whether all others are really wrong and only their own people or their own movement are in the right.... [What had to be done, therefore, was this:]

A multiplicity of different adversaries must always be com-
bined so that in the eyes of the masses of one's own supporters
the struggle is directed against only one enemy. This
strengthens their faith in their own right and enhances their
bitterness against those who attack it." [27]

The Nazis' attempt to diminish objectivity and to encourage
emotionalism was very similar to the tactics used by the
mountebanks of previous centuries. "The constant repetitions
of words and phrases in the charlatan's flood of babble,"
Grete de Francesco tells us, ". . .must have brought pleasure
instead of surfeit to the majority of auditors. . . . A slogan or
'catchword' must be simple, capable of endless repetition,
variable, and of an emotional breadth that permits each individual to attach his own private values to it. When all
these conditions are fulfilled, a shorthand sign may become
a whole program in itself." [28] The inexact use of words was
an integral part of the charlatans' and Nazis' persuasive
arsenal. "Exact words," said de Francesco, "make a demand upon the understanding; people must find themselves
in them. But one loses oneself in iridescent words, and that
was what both quack and crowd desired. Drunk on illusion,
the followers of the charlatan greedily absorbed his emotion-
soaked verbiage and most readily when he painted visions
of the future." [29]

So the savior-magician Hitler conjured up the "Jewish
disease" and the "Red Dragon," "das System" and the "November criminals," doing his best to keep objectivity from
interfering with persuasion. Objectivity and rational, intelligent descriptions of the reality of things had no place in
the Nazi persuasion and this in turn made unnecessary any
rational political and social answers to the problems facing
the German nation. The words Hitler used to "explain"
the plight of the Germans did not accurately describe things

or the relations of things. A semantically meaningful use of words would have been out of place in the ritual performances put on for the German people. So Hitler could declare in a speech delivered in Nuremberg in 1937: "This pestilence [Communism] will ask no man's permission to put an end to the democracies through the Marxist leadership, [and] it will do so without any man's leave, unless it meets with opposition. And this opposition must be something else than merely Platonic rejection of the doctrine, or any more or less solemn proclamation of hostility: there must be an immunization of the people against this poison while the international carrier of the bacillus must be fought." [30]

The Jew "is the demon of the disintegration of peoples, he is the symbol of the unceasing destruction of their life," [31] Hitler asserted in May, 1923. Comparing himself with Jesus Christ, Hitler said in an April 1922 speech that like Christ he too would drive out of the temple the "brood of vipers and adders." [32] In April 1939 he declared that "only when this Jewish bacillus infecting the life of peoples has been removed can one hope to establish a co-operation amongst the nations which shall be built up on a lasting understanding." [33]

The Nazis conjured up fantastic tales of Jewish demonology. It is difficult to understand how they could have been taken seriously by any intelligent, rational human being, but Hitler was dealing with a mentality susceptible to demons, dragons, and adders. According to the anti-Semitic publication *Der Stürmer*, the Jew was the demon who took blood from Aryan children and mixed it into his wine and bread. *Der Stürmer* fabricated reports about Jews who slaughtered Christians at the ritual celebrations of Passover: "The procedure is as follows: The family head empties a few drops of the fresh and powdered blood into a glass, wets the fingers

of the left hand with it, and sprays (blesses) with it everything on the table. The head of the family then says, 'Thus
we ask God to send the ten plagues to all the enemies of
the Jewish faith.' Then they eat, and at the end of the meal
the head of the family exclaims, 'May all Gentiles perish
as the child whose blood is contained in the bread and wine.'

"The fresh (or dried and powdered) blood of the slaughtered is further used by young Jewish couples, by pregnant
Jewish women, for circumcision, and so on. Ritual murder
is recognized by all Talmud Jews. The Jew believes he
absolves himself thus of his sins." [34]

For the German children there were stories on how to
identify Jews. One such story ended with the following
poem:

> The evil devil speaks to us
> Out of a Jewish face,
> The devil who in every land
> Is known as a wicked plague.
> If we want to be freed from Jews
> And be happy and gay again,
> Then the youth has to fight with us
> To conquer the Jewish devil. [35]

Admittedly, said the Nazis, the number of Jews in the
world is small, but then the power of the devil never was
dependent upon numerical strength. As the Nazis figured
it, the world's population was 0.3 percent Jewish, 15.7 percent Mohammedan, 30.6 percent Christian, and 53.4 percent heathen. How could 0.3 percent of the world's population have so much power over the remaining 99.7 percent?
If the Jews had been portrayed and defined as human beings
with human characteristics, human strengths and weaknesses,
it would have been obvious that they could have had little
power over so great a number of non-Jews. This 0.3 per-

cent had therefore to be defined as demonic, as having the power of the plague, as a disease capable of infecting and destroying whole populations.

The "Red Dragon" and the "Jewish bacillus" could not be destroyed, of course, with any sound political or social programs arrived at in parliamentary discussion and debate. To destroy the insidious evils — plague, demon, viper — the machinations and word magic of the medicine man, the magician, were needed. Having conjured up the evil phenomena, having directed the attention of the German populace to the fearful elements which besieged them, Hitler declared himself the savior-magician who alone could deliver them from demons and dragons. He was especially needed, the people were told, to destroy the micro-organisms, which were the most insidious, the most dangerous. As Lowenthal and Guterman have written: "The micro-organism seems to combine all the various enemy qualities in the highest degree. It is ubiquitous, close, deadly, insidious, it invites the idea of extermination, and, most important, it is invisible to the naked eye — the agitator expert is required to detect its presence." [36]

"Bolshevist poison," "Jewish bacillus," and "Red Dragon" were not mere figures of speech in the Nazi persuasion; defining human beings into "parasites," "disease," and "poison" was so consistently and vehemently done by the Nazis that these insidious and ubiquitous things became substitutes for perceiving human beings. If magic words were to be effective the "enemy" could not be simply a criminal or psychopath with human features for, in the words of Lowenthal and Guterman, "law and custom provide procedures for handling them. But the agitator breaks this tenuous link between the enemy and mankind by transforming him into a low animal." [38] The Bolsheviks were not *like* a dragon, they *were* a dragon; the Jews were not *like* a demon or bacillus, they *were* demon and bacillus.

The anxiety ridden Germans were psychologically ready to accept Hitler's explanation for their ill luck, their economic, social, and political turmoil. One of the functions of a society is to give its members a kind of security that makes living in community workable and enjoyable. Amid defeat in war, the violence of revolution, inflation, unemployment, and depression, the German nation under the Weimar Republic apparently did not give the people that security. In the words of theologian Paul Tillich: "A longing for security was growing in everybody. A freedom that leads to fear and anxiety has lost its virtue: better authority with security than freedom with fear!" [39]

So Adolf Hitler led the German people in their "escape from freedom." [40] He promised them security and replaced the feeling of powerlessness to cope with the "enemy" with action against it. Charles Odier has explained the relationship between the feeling of powerlessness in the anxiety ridden individual and his or her turn to magic: "Very often the feeling of powerlessness comes first, is primary. Having felt for so long belittled, completely stupid, crushed, and utterly incompetent, the subject experiences anxiety. Without realizing it, he then goes on from such feelings to the magic conviction of being surrounded and threatened by hostile forces which he will never be able to master. [This magic thinking and the anxiety] sooner or later produce what I should like to call the syndrome of ego dysfunction. There are three characteristics and related symptoms: feelings of helplessness, of insecurity, and of self-devaluation." [41]

These "symptoms" are strikingly close to the "feelings" which Tillich found prevailing in Germany and other western European countries in the 1930's. The cultural disintegration, said Tillich, expressed itself in four ways: fear, uncertainty, loneliness, and meaninglessness.

Instead of diagnosing the malaise in order to find politically and socially sound remedies, Hitler took advantage of it and used it to entice the Germans to make their "escape from freedom." He constantly reminded his audiences that the German people had been dishonored by the Treaty of Versailles, that they were looked upon as second class by the rest of the world, that they were helpless under democratic parliamentary government. All through the *Kampfzeit* Hitler aroused the populace to fear and hate the "diseases" of Bolshevism and Jewry. Even after he took power in 1933, Bolshevism may have been destroyed within the borders of Germany, but the "world plague" now threatened at the frontiers. The perpetual crisis was maintained. The devils and sorcerers still threatened. Hence, the words of the savior-magician were needed and the sure-fire magical potions would rid the land of the plague!

Torchlight parades through the streets of German cities would ward off the evils. The Nazi eagle would destroy the viper and adder. The sword would kill the dragon. Fire would wipe out the plague. Demonstrations of power and shouts of "Heil Hitler" would scare off the demons. The power of the *Blutfahne* (the "Blood-Flag" which purportedly had on it the blood of Nazis who had participated in the 1923 *putsch* and which was used to consecrate other Nazi banners) would attack the "blood contamination." And then the powerful magic words of him whom Destiny and Fate had sent would destroy the pestilence and the power of darkness. Those powerful words would, after all, destroy all evil, for he was — was he not? — the one chosen by Providence to awaken he German people. As claimed by various Nazis and by Hitler himself, God had revealed Himself to the German nation through Adolf Hitler.

Since ordinary men with ordinary powers working in ordinary parliaments could not successfully cope with the dragon and bacilli, there had to appear "heroes" to work miracles. And so they did. These heroes, chosen by Fate, appeared in the form of Hitler and his National Socialists. How did it happen? It came about in such a way that it would appear to posterity as a fairy tale, said Hitler. In a speech in Munich on the twelfth anniversary of the 1923 *putsch* he told his listeners about this "fairy tale," and in the process he brought into play many of the Nazi devices of persuasion — the miracle, the heroes, Fate, the unknown, the fanaticism and saga surrounding the Nazis, the blood of the martyrs, their resurrection. He described the development of the Nazi movement as "truly a miracle": "To posterity it will appear as a fairy tale. A people is shattered and then a small company of unknown men arises and begins an odyssey of wanderings which begins in fanaticism, pursues its course. Only a few years later and already from these few men, from these unknown, nameless folk, numerous battalions have been formed.... [The National Socialist movement] fights its fight on the streets. Thousands are wounded, but none the less the stream grows in volume, and the movement struggles through to power, and then it sets its standard over a whole state. A wonderful journey! History will record it as one of the most wonderful, one of the most remarkable happenings in the history of the world.... This is the miracle which we have wrought. We are the fortunate ones, for we need not learn the story from books; we have been chosen by fate to live this miracle in our own experience." [42]

The German people turned to this savior-magician, who came from the great unknown, chosen by Fate to bring miracles and resurrection to Germany, to free his followers from the demons which plagued them, because, to use the words of anthropologist Bronislaw Malinowski, "organized magic always appears within those domains of human activity where experience has demonstrated to man his pragmatic impotence." [43] Through the magic word, augumented with the nonverbal symbols of persuasion, Adolf Hitler led the German people away from discursive thinking and into a phantasmagoric world. "In desperate situations," writes Ernst Cassirer, "man will always have recourse to desperate means — and our present-day political myths have been such desperate means. If reason has failed us, there remains the *ultima* ratio, the power of the miraculous and mysterious." [44]

The distance between the linguistic dehumanization of a people and their actual suppression and extermination is not great; it is but a small step. Supreme Court Justice Robert Jackson said in another context: "Those who begin coercive elimination of dissent soon find themselves exterminating dissenters. Compulsory unification of opinion achieves only the unanimity of the graveyard." [45] Once Hitler had successfully defined the Jews into sub-humans, the decivilizing process was put into action. Restaurants displayed signs reading "Dogs and Jews Not Admitted." Signs at swimming pools and theaters read: "Jews Keep Out." Jewish shops and synagogues were destroyed while the police stood by. It was decreed in 1935 that "marriages between Jews and citizens of German or kindred blood are hereby forbidden. Marriages performed despite this ban are void, even if, to contravene the law, they were performed abroad." (See chapters on the "Language of White Racism" and "Defining the 'American Indian'" for application of similar miscegenation laws in the United States up into

the 1960's) It was further ordered that "extramarital intercourse between Jews and citizens of German or kindred
blood is forbidden." It was decreed in 1938 that "Jews
may receive only first names which are listed in the directives
of the Ministry of the Interior concerning the use of first
names." A 1941 Nazi decree stipulated that "Jews. . .over
the age of six are forbidden to show themselves in public
without a Jew's star."

Finally, the "Final Solution," the systematic extermination of a whole segment of humanity. Millions of Jews,
young and old, male and female, rich and poor, healthy and
sick, were loaded into cattle cars, riding sometimes for days
without food or water or toilet facilities, destined for the
concentration camps. The language of oppression and dehumanization followed the Jews into the camps: "The standard phrase used by SS record clerks for new arrivals at
Dachau was 'Which Jew-whore shit you out?' — a question
designed to elicit the name of the inmate's mother. At Belsen the female warders talked of handling so and so many
new 'pieces of prisoner per day' and the correspondence between IG-Farben's drug research section and the Auschwitz
camp authorities referred to 'loads' or 'consignments' of
human guinea-pigs." [46]

The "Final Solution" meant the gassing, cremation, and
shooting of six million Jews. To even speak, as we do, of
"six million Jews" killed distracts from the human element
involved in the deaths of so many human beings; "six million Jews" is too much an abstraction to convey any humanity. Those sent to their deaths were neither "demons,"
"vermin," "bacilli," nor an abstract "six million." They
were human beings with human aspirations, human desires,
human weaknesses, and human strengths. The perniciousness
of Hitler's language of oppression was that "the incessant

official demonization of the Jew gradually modified the consciousness even of naturally humane people," and by the
end of the Nazi regime the populace was indifferent to
Jewish sufferings, "not because it occurred in wartime and
under conditions of secrecy, but because Jews were astro-
nomically remote and not real people." [47]

Once an oppressed segment of humanity has been redefined
in the manner that the Jews were redefined we should not
be surprised at the resultant inhumanity, degradation, and
death. If unchecked, the logical extension of the language
of oppression is what happened, as reported by a German
eyewitness, to hundreds of Jews in a field in Poland on
October 5, 1942:

"The people from the trucks — men, women, and children — were forced to undress under the supervision of an
SS (Nazi Storm Trooper) soldier with a whip in his hand. . . .
I saw a pile of shoes, about 800-1000 pairs, great heaps of
underwear and clothing. Without weeping or crying out
these people undressed and stood together in family groups,
embracing each other and saying goodby. . . . During the
fifteen minutes I stayed there, I did not hear a single com-
plaint or a plea for mercy. I watched a family of about eight:
a man and woman about fifty years old, surrounded by their
children of about one, eight and ten, and two big girls about
twenty and twenty-four. An old lady, her hair completely
white, held the baby in her arms, rocking it and singing it a
song. The infant was crying aloud with delight. The parents
watched the group with tears in their eyes. The father held
the ten-year-old boy by the hand, speaking softly to him;
the child struggled to hold back his tears. Then the father
pointed a finger to the sky and stroking the child's head
seemed to be explaining something. At this moment the SS
near the ditch called something to his comrade. The latter

counted off some twenty people and ordered them behind
the mound. I still remember the young girl, slender and
dark, who, passing near me, pointed to herself, saying 'twenty-
three.' I walked around the mound and faced a frightful
common grave. . . . The ditch was two-thirds full. I estimate that it held a thousand bodies." [48]

3

THE LANGUAGE OF WHITE RACISM

Attempts to eradicate racism in the United States have been focused notably on the blacks of America, not on the whites. What is striking is that while we have been inundated with television programs portraying the plight of the blacks, and with panel discussions focusing on black Americans, we very seldom have heard or seen any extensive public dialogue, literature or programs directly related to the source of the racism — the white American.

We have seen on our television sets and in our periodicals pictures and descriptions of undernourished black children, but we have seldom seen pictures or been presented with analyses of the millions of white suburban children being taught racism in their white classrooms; we have seen pictures of unemployed blacks aimlessly walking the streets in their black communities, but seldom have we seen exposed the whites who have been largely responsible, directly or indirectly, for this unemployment and segregation; we have heard the panelists discussing and diagnosing the blacks in the nation, but seldom have we heard panelists diagnosing the whites and their subtle and not so subtle racism.

Gunnar Myrdal, in the introduction to his classic work *An American Dilemma*, tells us that as he "proceeded in his studies into the Negro problem [an unfortunate phrase which will be discussed later] it became increasingly evident that little, if anything, could be scientifically explained in terms of the peculiarities of the Negroes themselves." [1] It is the white majority group, said Myrdal, "that naturally determines the Negro's 'place.' All our attempts to reach scientific explanations of why the Negroes are what they are and why they live as they do have regularly led to determinants on the white side of the race line." As an *Ebony* editorial put the matter in 1966, "for too long now, we have focused on the symptoms of the disease rather than the disease itself. It is time now for us to face the fact that Negroes are oppressed in America not by 'the pathology of the ghetto,' as some experts contend, but by the pathology of the white community." In calling for a White House Conference on whites, *Ebony* made the important point that "we need to know more about the pathology of the white community. We need conferences in which white leaders will talk not about us but about themselves." [2]

White Americans, through the mass media and individually, must begin to focus their attention not on the condition of the victimized, but on the victimizer. Whites must begin to take the advice of black spokespersons who suggest that white Americans start solving the racial strife in this country by eradicating white racism in white communities, instead of going into black communities or joining black organizations to "give" the blacks political and social rights. This suggestion has come from Floyd McKissick, Malcolm X, and Stokely Carmichael.

McKissick, when asked what the role of the whites was in the blacks' struggle, answered: "If there are whites who are not racists, I believe there are a few, a *very* few, let them go to their own communities and teach; teach white people the truth about the black man." [3] Malcolm X wrote in his autobiography: "The Negroes aren't the racists. Where the really sincere white people have to do their 'proving' of themselves is not among the black *victims*, but out on the battle lines of where America's racism really *is* — and that's in their own home communities; America's racism is among their own whites. That's where the sincere whites who really mean to accomplish something have to work." [4] Stokely Carmichael, writing in the September 22, 1966 issue of *The New York Review*, said that "one of the most disturbing things about almost all white supporters of the movement has been that they are afraid to go into their own communities — which is where the racism exists — and work to get rid of it." [5]

An important step in that direction which most whites can take is to clean up their language by getting rid of words and phrases which connote racism to the blacks. Whereas many blacks have demonstrated an increased sensitivity to language and an awareness of the impact of words and phrases upon both black and white listeners, the whites of the nation have demonstrated little sensitivity to the language of racial strife. Whitey has been for too long speaking and writing in terminology which, often being offensive to the blacks, creates hostility, suspicions, and barriers to communication. Through the language of white racism the races have been "separated," the blacks linguistically designated subjects in the master-subject relationship.

From the moment black Africans were forcibly transported to Virginia early in the seventeenth century to be used as slaves, their identity, their self-perception, their being, was controlled by the white masters. As John Oliver Killens has correctly observed: "In order to justify slavery in a courageous new world which was spouting slogans of freedom and equality and brotherhood, the enslavers, through their propagandists, had to create the fiction that the enslaved people were subhuman and undeserving of human rights and sympathies. The first job was to convince the outside world of the inherent inferiority of the enslaved. The second job was to convince the American people. And the third job, which was the cruelist hoax of all, was to convince the slaves themselves that they deserved to be slaves." [6]

The process of creating the fiction of the "subhuman" character of blacks was brought by the colonists from England and quickly applied to justify the oppression and enslavement of the blacks. Winthrop Jordan has pointed out in his work *White Over Black,* the English identified the "Negroes" as heathens: "Indeed the most important aspect of English reaction to Negro heathenism was that Englishmen evidently did not regard it as separable from the Negro's other attributes. Heathenism was treated not so much as a specifically religious defect but as one manifestation of a general refusal to measure up to proper standards, as a failure to be English or even civilized." [7]

In addition to being defined as heathens, the blacks were dubbed "savages," but as Jordan explains, the English knew perfectly well "that Negroes were men, yet they frequently described the Africans as 'brutish' or 'bestial' or 'beastly.' The hideous tortures, the cannibalism, the rapacious warfare, the revolting diet (and so forth page after page) seemed somehow to place the Negro among the beasts." The blacks were then likened to "apes" and as "apes" they were, or course, "animalistic." [8] This "animalism was linked with beastly sexuality: "It is no accident that this affinity between Negroes and apes was so frequently regarded as sexual, for undertones of sexuality run throughout many English accounts of West Africa. To liken Africans — any human beings — to beasts was to stress the animal within the man." [9] Having defined the blacks as uncivilized, heathens, barbarians, apes, and animals, it was an easy step to oppress them into slavery. As "animals" they could be transported to the colonies like animals. "During the dreaded 'Middle Passage' across the Atlantic, whenever the shipmaster had to preserve the safety of the ship, he did not hesitate to jettison his human cargo. Legal definitions to cover such contingencies became a necessity; and for insurance purposes the men, women, and children thrown to the sharks were designated as goods or chattels." [10]

The language of the law was brought to bear to designate the blacks as "nonpersons," as less than civilized. The famous Dred Scott decision of 1857 was one of the many court rulings which helped institutionalize racism by defining blacks as having no rights as human beings. Referring to the Dred Scott decision and Supreme Court Chief Justice Taney's opinion in *Dred Scott v. Sanford*, 60 U. S. 363 (1857), Derrick Bell, Jr. wrote that Taney's "well-documented argument as to the status of black people in this country stands as an irrefutable testament to the extension of the nation's belief in the inferiority of blacks, and the degree to which those beliefs had been inculcated into the laws of the land." [11]

In declaring that no Negro, free or slave, could be considered a citizen of the United States, Justice Taney wrote:

"The words 'people of the United States' and 'citizens' are synonymous terms, and mean the same thing. They both describe the political body who, according to our republican institutions, form the sovereignty, and who hold the power and conduct the Government through their representatives. They are what we familiarly call the 'sovereign people,' and every citizen is one of this people, and a constituent member of this sovereignty. The question before us is, whether the class of persons described in the plea in abatement compose a portion of this people, and are constituent members of this sovereignty? We think

they are not included, and were not intended to be included, under the word 'citizens' in the Constitution, and can
therefore claim none of the rights and privileges which that
instrument provides for and secures to citizens of the
United States. On the contrary, they were at that time
considered as a subordinate and inferior class of beings,
who had been subjugated by the dominant race, and, whether
emancipated or not, yet remained subject to their authority,
and had no rights or privileges but such as those who
held the power and the Government might choose to grant
them." [12]

The statement in the Declaration of Independence saying that "all men are created equal" was never meant,
Justice Taney held, to include Negroes and that "the only
provisions [in the Constitution] which point to them and
include them, treat them as property, and make it the
duty of the Government to protect it." [13]

During the eighteenth and nineteenth centuries scores
of state statutes were enacted to keep the "superior" whites
separated from the "inferior" blacks. A variety of miscegenation laws, for example, were passed by legislatures
to prohibit social and physical intercourse between whites
and blacks. "Before the American Revolution, at least five
states had established legislative bans and penalties against
inter-racial marriage and/or cohabitation." [14] In a brief
discussion of miscegenation laws, the April 1927 issue of
the *Yale Law Review* indicated that "the statutes prohibiting intermarriage between white persons and Negroes
vary widely in their definition of 'Negro.'" [15] The article
noted the inability of legislatures to agree on who was a
"Negro":

"Some of the statutes prohibit marriages between white
persons and persons of African descent (Georgia, Okla-

homa, Texas), or between white persons and persons of
Negro blood to the third generation (Alabama, Mary-
land, North Carolina, Tennessee), or between white persons and persons of more than one-fourth (Oregon, West
Virginia), or one-eighth (Virginia) Negro blood; other
statutes in more general terms prohibit marriages between
white persons and Negroes or mulattoes (Arkansas, Colorado, Delaware, Idaho, Kentucky, Louisiana, Missouri,
Montana, Nevada, South Carolina, South Dakota, Utah,
Wyoming)." [16]

In 1955 more than half the states still had miscegenation
statutes. It was not until 1966 that the United States Supreme Court declared unconstitutional statutes forbidding
marriages between persons solely on the basis of racial
classifications.

The numerous court opinions which upheld miscegenation laws argued that this separation of the races constituted legitimate efforts of states to maintain the morals
and civilization of a people; in some cases, judges argued
that the miscegenation statutes did not discriminate and
were not violations of the Fourteenth Amendment since
both offenders, black and white, were given the same
punishment for their crime of intermarriage. In 1882
the United States Supreme Court dealt with two Alabama
statutes related to adultery, fornication, and miscegenation.
Tony Pace, a black, and Mary Cox, a white, were indicted
under Section 4189 of the Alabama Code which stipulated
that "if any white person and any Negro, or the descendant
of any Negro to the third generation, inclusive, though
one ancestor of each generation was a white person, intermarry or live in adultery or fornication with each other,
each of them must, on conviction, be imprisoned in the
penitentiary or sentenced to hard labor for the county

for not less than two nor more than seven years."

The highest court in the land upheld the convictions, stating that Section 4184 prohibiting adultery and fornication and Section 4189 were not violations of the Fourteenth Amendment of the United States Constitution which guarantees that no State shall "deny to any person the equal protection of the laws." In so deciding the Court declared: "There is in neither section any discrimination against either race. Sect. 4189 applies the same punishment to both offenders, the white and the black. Indeed, the offense against which this latter section is aimed cannot be committed without involving the persons of both races in the same punishment. Whatever discrimination is made in the punishment prescribed in the two sections is directed against the offense designated and not against the person or any particular color or race. The punishment of each offending person, whether white or black, is the same." [17]

In 1944 the Circuit Court of Appeals, Tenth Circuit, used the same argument in upholding the constitutionality of an Oklahoma miscegenation statute which "forbids the marriage of any person of African descent, as defined in the constitution of the state, to any person not of such descent, or the marriage of any person not of African descent to a person of such descent; and section 13 provides that a marriage in violation of the preceding section shall be deemed a felony and punished as therein specified." [18] The Circuit Court took the position that "the statute does not merely forbid a person of African descent to intermarry with a person of other race or descent. It equally forbids a person of other race or descent to intermarry with a person of African descent. And the succeeding section prescribes the same punishment for both offenders. There is no discrimination against the colored race." [19]

In rejecting the argument that the Oklahoma statute was a violation of the Fourteenth Amendment the court declared: "Marriage is a consentient covenant. It is a contract in the sense that it is entered into by agreement of the parties. But it is more than a civil contract between them, subject to their will and pleasure in respect of effects, continuance, or dissolution. It is a domestic relation having to do with the morals and civilization of a people. It is an essential institution in every well organized society. It affects in a vital manner public welfare, and its control and regulation is a matter of domestic concern within each state." [20] One of the unusual elements of this decision was the defining of "a full-blood Creek Indian" as a white person; Stella Sands, the Creek Indian, not of African descent, married William Stevens who was of African descent.

What made Stella Sands a part of the "white race" was Article XXIII, Section 11, of the Oklahoma Constitution which provided "that wherever in the constitution and laws of the state the word or words 'colored' or 'colored race.' 'negro' or 'negro race,' are used, it or they shall be construed to mean and apply to all persons of African descent, and that the term 'white race' shall include all other persons." The anomaly of this unusual 1944 decision lay in the fact that almost all other courts across the land had designated the "Indian race" as separate from the "white race," claiming that "it is a well-known fact that Indians as a race are not as highly civilized as the whites." (See Chapter 4).

In 1955 the Supreme Court of Appeals of Virginia upheld the constitutionality of that state's "Act to preserve racial integrity," a statute reading: "It shall hereafter be unlawful for any white person in this State to marry any save a white person, or a person with no other admixture of blood than white and American Indian. For the purpose of this chapter, the term 'white person' shall apply only to such person as has no trace whatever of any blood other than Caucasian; but persons who have one-sixteenth or less of the blood of the American Indian and have no other non-Caucasic blood shall be deemed to be white persons." The Virginia court held that the marriage of a "white person" and a "Chinese" was void, a finding which would have been equally applied in the case of a marriage between a white and a black person. In its opinion the court spoke of the state's interest in regulating public health and the "physical, moral and spiritual well-being of its citizens."

Then the court turned to the subjects of "racial integrity," "racial pride," and the "mongrel breed": "We are unable to read in the Fourteenth Amendment to the Constitution, or in any other provision of that great document, any words or any intendment which prohibit the State from enacting legislation to preserve the racial integrity of its citizens, or which denies the power of the State to regulate the marriage relation so that it shall not have a mongrel breed of citizens. We find there no requirement that the State shall not legislate to prevent the obliteration of racial pride, but must permit the corruption of blood even though it weaken or destroy the quality of its citizenship. Both sacred and secular history teach that nations and races have better advanced in human progress when they cultivated their own distinctive characteristics and culture and developed their own peculiar genius." [21]

Finally, in 1966, a century after the Civil War, two centuries after the Declaration of Independence, and three centuries after slavery was recognized as legal in Virginia, the United States Supreme Court concluded that Virginia's laws prohibiting interracial marriages were unconstitutional. The Court provided the following background information: "In June 1958, two residents of Virginia, Mildred Jeter, a Negro woman, and Richard Loving, a white man, were married in the District of Columbia pursuant to its laws. Shortly after their marriage, the Lovings returned to Virginia and established their marital abode in Caroline County. At the October Term, 1958, of the Circuit Court of Caroline County, a grand jury issued an indictment charging the Lovings with violating Virginia's ban on interracial marriages.

"On January 6, 1959, the Lovings pleaded guilty to the charge and were sentenced to one year in jail; the trial judge, however, suspended the sentence for a period of 25 years on the condition that the Lovings leave the State and not return to Virginia together for 25 years. He stated in an opinion that: 'Almighty God created the races white, black, yellow, malay, and red, and he placed them on separate continents. And but for the interference with this arrangement there would be no cause for such marriages. The fact that he separated the races shows that he did not intend for the races to mix.' " [22]

The Lovings appealed to the Supreme Court of Appeals of Virginia which upheld the convictions and the constitutionality of the statutes. In 1966, however, the United States Supreme Court reversed. Chief Justice Earl Warren spoke for the Court: "There is patently no legitimate overriding purpose independent of invidious racial discrimination which justifies this classification. The fact that Virginia prohibits only interracial marriages involving white persons demonstrates that the racial classifications must stand on their own justification, as measures designed to maintain White Supremacy." [23]

The hundreds of state statutes and court opinions up to

the middle of the twentieth century attempted to keep the "superior" race separated from the "inferior" races. The races were kept apart through enforcement of segregated housing, segregated schools, segregated eating facilities, segregated entertainment facilities, separated drinking fountains, separated library facilities, separated military units, separated cemeteries. The language of the legislators and judges, their phrases "to preserve the racial integrity," "to prevent a mongrel breed of citizens," "to prevent the obliteration of racial pride," contributed to the separation and isolation of racial communities.

As Anthony Downs has pointed out, "separation of groups is one of the oldest and most widespread devices for subordination in all societies." [24] One has only to compare Hitler's miscegenation laws for "the protection of German blood" with those enforced in over half the states in the United States at the time it was at war against the Nazis. Nazi law proclaimed: "Marriages between Jews and citizens of German or kindred blood are hereby forbidden. Marriages performed despite this ban are void, even if, to contravene the law, they were performed abroad." Substitute "Negroes" for "Jews" and "white" for "German" and you have the law of more than half the states circa 1955.

There appeared in the 1960's a significant increase in awareness on the part of black Americans of the impact of language, legal and otherwise, on how others saw them and how they saw themselves. More black speakers and writers began referring to the "Through the Looking Glass" episode where Humpty Dumpty says: "When I use a word it means just what I choose it to mean — neither more nor less." "The question is," said Alice, "whether you can make words mean so many different things." "The question is," said Humpty Dumpty, "which is to be master — that's all." As a civil rights activist during the 1960's, Stokely Carmichael delivered a number of speeches in which he emphasized the importance of a people to be able to define themselves, not to be defined by others.

Speaking to students at Morgan State College on January 16, 1967, Carmichael said that "the need of a free people is to be able to define their own terms and have those terms recognized by their oppressors. It is also the first need that all oppressors must suspend." "And so," he continued, "for white people to be allowed to define us by calling us Negroes, which means apathetic, lazy, stupid, and all those other things, it is for us to accept those definitions. We must define what we are and move from our definitions and tell them to recognize what we are." Carmichael prefaced a retelling of the above Lewis Carroll tale with: "It [definition] is very, very important because I believe that people who can define are masters."

Carmichael went on to declare to his audience: "So I say 'black power' and someone says 'you mean violence.' And they expect me to say, 'no, no. I don't mean violence, I don't mean that.' Later for you; I am master of my own terms. If black power means violence to you, that is your problem. . . . I know what it means in my mind. I will stand clear and you must understand that because the first need of a free people is to be able to define their own terms and have those terms recognized by their oppressors. . . . Camus says that when a slave says 'no' he begins to exist." [25]

The "Through the Looking Glass" episode was used by Lerone Bennett, Jr. in the November 1967 issue of *Ebony* to introduce his article dealing with whether black Americans should call themselves "Negroes," "Blacks," or "Afro-Americans." This concern for words and names and their implications in race relations was voiced also by Martin Luther

King who pointed out that "even semantics have conspired to make that which is black seem ugly and degrading." [26] Writing in his last book before his death, *Where Do We Go From Here: Chaos or Community?*, King said: "In Roget's Thesaurus there are some 120 synonyms for 'blackness' and at least 60 of them are offensive — such words as 'blot,' 'soot,' 'grime,' 'devil,' and 'foul.' There are some 134 synonyms for 'whiteness' and all are favorable, expressed in such words as 'purity,' 'cleanliness,' 'chastity,' and 'innocence.' A white lie is better than a black lie. The most degenerate member of the family is the 'black sheep,' not the 'white sheep.'" [27]

In March 1962, *The Negro History Bulletin* published an article by L. Eldridge Cleaver, then imprisoned in San Quentin, who devoted several pages to a discussion of the black American's acceptance of a white society's standards for beauty and to an analysis of the negative connotations of the word "black" and the positive connotations of the word "white." Cleaver told black Americans that "what we must do is stop associating the Caucasian with these exalted connotations of the word *white* when we think or speak of him. At the same time, we must cease associating ourselves with the unsavory connotations of the word black." [28]

Cleaver made an interesting point when he brought to his readers' attention the term "non-white": "The very words that we use indicate that we have set a premium on the Caucasian ideal of beauty. When discussing inter-racial relations, we speak of 'white people' and 'non-white people.' Notice that that particular choice of words gives precedence to 'white people' by making them a center — a standard — to which 'non-white' bears a negative relation. Notice the different connotations when we turn around and say 'colored' and 'non-colored,' or 'black' or 'non-black.' " [29]

Simon Podair, writing in a 1965 issue of *Phylon*, examined the connotations of such words as "blackmail," "blacklist," "blackbook," "blacksheep," and "blackball." The assertion made by Podair that it has been white civilization which has attributed to the word "black" things undesirable and evil warrants brief examination. He is correct when he asserts that "language as a potent force in our society goes beyond being merely a communicative device. Language not only expresses ideas and concepts but it may actually shape them. Often the process is completely unconscious with the individual concerned unaware of the influence of the spoken or written expressions upon his thought processes. Language can thus become an instrument of both propaganda and indoctrination for a given idea." [30]

Further, Podar is correct in saying that "so powerful is the role of language in its imprint upon the human mind that even the minority group may begin to accept the very expressions that aid in its stereotyping. Thus, even Negroes may develop speech patterns filled with expressions leading to the strengthening of stereotypes." [31] This point was illustrated by the comments made by a black state official in Washington upon hearing of the shooting of Robert Kennedy. The Director of the Washington State Board Against Discrimination said: "This is a black day in our country's history." Immediately after uttering this statement with the negative connotation of "black," he declared that Robert Kennedy "is a hero in the eyes of black people — a champion of the oppressed — and we all pray for his complete recovery." [32]

Although King, Cleaver, and Podair, and others concerned with the negative connotations of "black" in the white society are partially correct in their analysis, they have omitted in their discussions two points which by their omission effect an incomplete analysis. First, it is not quite accurate to say, as Podair has, that the concepts of black as hostile, foreboding, wicked, and gloomy "cannot be considered accidental and undoubtedly would not exist in a society wherein whites were a minority. Historically, these concepts have evolved as a result of the need of the dominant group to maintain social and economic relationships on the basis of inequality if its hegemony was to survive." This is inaccurate because the terms "blackmail," "blacklist," "blackbook," and "blackball" did not evolve as "a result of the need of the dominant group to maintain social and economic relationships on the basis of inequality if its hegemony was to survive."

The origins of such terms are to be found in the sixteenth and seventeenth centuries in England where the words and phrases were mostly based on the color of the book cover, the color of printing, or the color of the object from which the word got its meaning, as for instance the term "to blackball" coming from "the black ball" which centuries ago was a vote against a person or thing. A "blackletter day" had its origin in the eighteenth century to designate an inauspicious day, as distinguished from a "red letter day," the reference being to the old custom of marking the saint's days in the calendar with red letters.

More important, the assertion that the negative connotations of "black" and the positive connotations of "white" would not exist in a society wherein whites were a minority is not accurate. Centuries ago, before black societies ever saw white persons, "black" often had negative connotations, and "white" positive in those societies. In his article 'Swazi Royal Ritual," published in the October 1966 issue of *Africa*, T. O. Beidelman makes it clear that black societies in southeast Africa, while attributing to black positive qualities, can at the same time attribute to black negative qualities; the same applies to the color white. Beidelman writes that for the Swazi "darkness, as the 'covered' moon, is an ambiguous quality. Black symbolizes 'impenetrability of the future,' but also the 'sins and evils of the past year.' " [33] Black beads may symbolize marriage and wealth in cattle, but at the same time they can symbolize evil, disappointment, and misfortune. "The word *mnyama* means black and dark, but also means deep, profound, unfathomable, and even confused, dizzy, angry." To the Swazi, "that which is dark is unknown and ambiguous and dangerous, but it is also profound, latent with unknown meanings and possibilities." As for "white," *mhlophe* means to the Swazi "white, pale, pure, innocent, perfect, but this may also mean destitute and empty. The whiteness of the full moon, *inyanga isidindile*, relates to fullness; but this term *dinda* can also mean to be useless, simply because it refers to that which is fully exposed and having no further unknown potentialities." [34]

What King, Cleaver, and Podair have failed to do in their discussions of the negative connotations of "black" and the positive of "white" is to point out that in black societies "black" often connotes that which is hostile, foreboding, and gloomy and "white" has symbolized purity and divinity. Furthermore, in white societies, "white" has numerous negative connotations: white livered (cowardly), white flag (surrender), white elephant (useless), white plague (tuberculosis), white wash (conceal), white feather (cowardice), et cetera. The ugliness and terror associated with the color white are portrayed by Melville in the chapter "The Whiteness of the Whale" in *Moby Dick*. At the beginning of the chapter Melville says: "It was the whiteness of the whale that above all things appalled me."

What is beng suggested here is that the black writers and speakers, while legitimately concerned with the words and phrases which perpetuate racism in the United States, have presented a partial analysis. This is not to say, however, that most of the analysis is not valid as far as it goes. Podair is entirely correct when he writes: "In modern American life language has become a fulcrum of prejudice as regards Negro-white relationships. Its effect has been equally potent upon the overt bigot as well as the confused member of the public who is struggling to overcome conscious or unconscious hostility towards minority groups. In the case of the Negro, language concepts have supported misconceptions and disoriented the thinking of many on the question of race and culture." [35] Not only has the black become trapped by these "language concepts," but so too have the whites who, unlike the blacks, have demonstrated very little insight into the language of white racism and whose "language concepts" have "supported misconceptions and disoriented the thinking of many on the question of race and culture."

The blacks' increased understanding and sensitivity to language as it is related to them demands that white Americans follow suit with similar understanding and sensitivity which they have not yet demonstrated too well. During the 1960's, at a time when black Americans were attempting more than ever to communicate to whites through speeches, marches, sit-ins, demonstrations, through violence and non-violence, the barriers of communication between blacks and whites seemed to be almost as divisive as they had been in the past one hundred years, no thanks to the whites.

One had only to watch the television panelists, blacks and whites, discussing the black American's grievances, protests, and aspirations, to see the facial expressions of the black panelists when a white on the panel spoke of "our colored boys in Vietnam." "Our colored boys in Vietnam" is a close relation to "our colored people" and "our colored" and "our colored folks," phrases which communicate more to the black American listener than intended by the white speaker. John Howard Griffin has pointed out something that applies not only to Southern whites, but to white Americans generally: "A great many of us Southern whites have grown up using an expression that Negroes can hardly bear to hear and yet tragically enough we use it because we believe it. It's an expression that we use when we say how much we love, what we patronizingly call 'our Negroes.' "[36] The white American who talks of "our colored boys in Vietnam" offends the blacks triply. First, by referring to the black American men as "our" which is, as Griffin points out, patronizing; second, by using the nineteenth century term "colored" which is so closely associated with the plantation and slavery; third, by referring to black American men as "boys."

Most whites, if not all, know that "nigger" and "boy" are offensive to blacks; in fact, such language could be classified as "fighting words," that is, words which would "have a direct tendency to cause acts of violence by the persons to whom, individually, the remark is addressed." But the insensitive and offensive whites have continued to indulge in expressing their overt and covert prejudices by using these obviously derogatory terms. In one of several articles on racism in athletics, *Sports Illustrated* quoted a black football player as saying "The word was never given bluntly; usually it took the form of a friendly, oblique talk with one of the assistant coaches. I remember one time one of the coaches came to me and said,'[Head Coach] Jim Owens loves you boys. We know you get a lot of publicity, but don't let it go to your head.' Hell, when he said 'Jim Owens loves you boys,' I just shut him off. That did it. I knew what he was talking about." [37]

One of the black athletes said of the coaching personnel at the same university: "They can pronounce Negro if they want to. *They can pronounce it.* But I think it seems like such a little thing to them. The trouble with them is they're not thinking of the Negro and how he feels. Wouldn't you suppose that if there was one word these guys that live off Negroes would get rid of, one single word in the whole vocabulary, it would be nigger?" [39] When a reporter tried to get the attention of Elvin Hayes, star basketball player at the University of Houston, the newsman shouted, "Hey boy!" Hayes turned to the reporter and said: "Boy's on *Tarzan.* I'm no boy. I'm 22 years old. I worked hard to become a man. I don't call you boy." The reporter apologized and said: "I didn't mean anything by it." [40] That excuse will no longer do.

Joel Kovel has provided the following explanation for the whites' past insistence to label mature black men as "boys": "In the classic South — and, as the fantasies generated there have diffused, throughout America — the sex fantasy has been incorporated into the white assumption of superiority and the demand for black submission. Whenever a black man bowed and scraped, whenever a white man called a black man 'boy,' or in other ways infantilized him, just below the surface of the white man's consciousness, a sexual fantasy would be found yoked to the symbol of power and status. These sex fantasies erupted whenever the power relationships were threatened. In the colonies the slightest rumor of a slave revolt was accompanied by wild

stories of blacks working their ultimate revenge in whole-
sale rapes of white women. Nor should anyone think that,
below the surface of reasonable concern, the fears aroused
in whites by the current black rebellion are different." [14]
Defining the mature black male as "boy" has been just one
more way for whites, especially insecure white males, to
emasculate the black, to minimize his "manliness." The
white oppressor, through this language of racism, forced
the black into a posture of subordination.

Whites who would never think of referring to blacks as
"boy" or "nigger" do, however, reveal themselves through
less obviously racist language. A day does not go by without
one hearing, from people who should know better, about
"the Negro problem," a phrase which carries with it the
implication that the Negro is a problem. One is reminded
of the Nazis talking about "the Jewish problem." There was
no Jewish problem! Yet the phrase carried the implication
that the Jews were a problem in Germany and hence being a
problem invited a solution and the solution Hitler proposed
and carried out was the "Final Solution." Even the most
competent writers fall into the "Negro problem" trap; James
Reston of the *New York Times* wrote on April 7, 1968:
"When Gunnar Myrdal, the Swedish social philosopher who
has followed the Negro problem in American for forty years,
came back recently, he felt that a great deal had changed
for the better, but concluded that we have greatly under-
estimated the scope of the Negro problem."

Myrdal himself titled his 1944 classic work *The American
Dilemma: The Negro Problem and Modern Democracy.* A
book published in 1967, *The Negro in 20th Century America,*
by John Hope Franklin and Isidore Starr, starts off its table
of contents with "Book One: *The Negro Problem*"; the foreword opens with: "The Negro problem was selected because

it is one of the great case studies in man's never-ending fight for equal rights." One of the selections in the book, a debate in which James Baldwin participates, has Baldwin's debate opponent saying that "the Negro problem is a very complicated one."

There are several indications that from here on out the black American is no longer going to accept the phrase "The Negro problem." As Lerone Bennett, Jr. said in the August 1965 issue of *Ebony*, "there is no Negro problem in America. The problem of race in America, insofar as that problem is related to packets of melanin in men's skins, is a white problem." In 1966 the editors of *Ebony* published a book of essays on American black-white relations entitled *The White Problem in America*. It is difficult to imagine blacks sitting around during the next decade talking about "the Negro problem," just as it is difficult to imagine Jews in 1939 referring to themselves as "the Jewish problem."

The racial brainwashing of whites in the United States leads them to utter such statements as "You don't sound like a Negro" or "Well, he didn't sound like a Negro to me." John Howard Griffin, who changed the color of his skin from white to black to find out what it meant to be black in America, was ashamed to admit that he thought he could not pass for a Negro because he "didn't know how to speak Negro."

"There is an illusion in this land," said Griffin, "that unless you sound as though you are reading Uncle Remus you couldn't possibly have an authentic Negro dialect. But I don't know what we've been using for ears because you don't have to be in the Negro community five minutes before the truth strikes and the truth is that there are just as many speech patterns in the Negro community as there are in any other, particularly in areas of rigid segregation where your right shoulder may be touching the shoulder of a Negro PhD. and your left shoulder the shoulder of the disadvantaged." [42]

A black American, when told that he or she does not "sound like a Negro," legitimately can ask the white conversationalist, "What does a Negro sound like?" This will probably place the white in a dilemma for one will either have to admit that sounding "like a Negro" means sounding like Prissy in *Gone With the Wind* ("Who dat say who dat when you say who dat?") or perhaps there is no such thing as "sounding like a Negro."

Goodman Ace, writing in the July 27, 1968 issue of the *Saturday Review,* pointed out that some years ago radio program planners attempted to write blacks into the radio scripts by portraying them as something else besides janitors, household maids, and train porters. Someone suggested that in the comedy radio show *Henry Aldrich* Henry might have among his friends a young black youth, without belaboring the point that he was black. As Ace observers, "just how it would be indicated on radio that the boy is black was not mentioned. Unless he was to be named Rufus or Rastus." Unless, it might be added, he was made to "sound like a Negro."

Psychiatrist Frantz Fanon, who begins his *Black Skin, White Masks* with a chapter entitled "The Negro and Language," explains the manner of many whites when talking to blacks and the effects of this manner. Although he is writing about white Europeans, what Fanon says applies equally to white Americans. He points out that most whites "talk down" to the Negro, and this "talking down" is, in effect, telling the black person, "You'd better keep your place." He writes: "A white man addressing a Negro behaves exactly like an adult with a child and starts smirking, whispering, patronizing, cozening." [43]

The effect of the whites' manner of speaking to the black "makes him angry, because he himself is a pidgin-nigger-talker." Fanon adds: "But I will be told there is no wish, no intention to anger him. I grant this; but it is just this absence of wish, this lack of interest, this indifference, this automatic manner of classifying him, imprisoning him, primitivizing him, decivilizing him, that makes him angry." [44] If a doctor greets his Negro patient with "You not feel good, no?" or "G'morning pal. Where's it hurt? Huh? Lemme see — belly ache? Heart pain?" the doctor feels perfectly justified in speaking that way, declares Fanon, when in return the patient answers in the same fashion; the doctor can then say to himself, "You see? I wasn't kidding you. That's just the way they are." To make the black talk pidgin, Fanon observes, "is to fasten him to the effigy of him, to snare him, to imprison him, the eternal victim of an essence, of an *appearance* for which he is not responsible. And naturally, just as a Jew who spends money without thinking about it is suspect, a black man who quotes Montesquieu had better be watched." [45]

The whites, in effect, encourage and perpetuate the stereotypes of blacks through the manner in which they speak about and to them. And if Fanon is correct, the whites, by "talking down" to the blacks, are telling the black American citizen to "remember where you come from!" The "talking down" and the infantilizing of blacks through the language of racism has its impact: "The patronizing attitude is really more damning than the competitive struggle. The stone wall of calm assumption of his inferiority is to the Negro a keener hurt and a greater obstacle than the battle which admits an adversary worth fighting against. It is hard to keep ambition alive and to maintain morale when those for whom you have fondness and respect keep thinking and saying that you are only children, that you can never grow up, that you are cast by God in an inferior mold." [46]

Another facet of the racism of the whites' language is reflected in their habit of referring to talented and great writers, athletes, entertainers, politicians, and clergy as "a great Negro singer" or "a great black poet" or "a great Negro ball player." What need is there for whites to designate the color or race of the person who has excelled? Paul Robeson and Marion Anderson are great and talented singers. James Baldwin and Leroi Jones are talented writers. Why must the greatness of these individuals be qualified in any way with "black" or "colored" or "Negro?" Fanon briefly refers to this predilection of whites to speak with qualification: "... Charles-André Julien introducing Aimé Césaire as a 'Negro poet with a university degree,' or again, quite simply, the expression, 'a great black poet.'

"These ready-made phrases, which seem in a common-sense way to fill a need — Aimé Césaire is really black and a poet — have a hidden subtlety, a permanent rub. I know nothing of Jean Paulham except that he writes very interesting books; I have no idea how old Roger Caillois is, since the only evidence I have of his existence are the books of his that streak across my horizon. And let no one accuse me of affective allergies; what I am trying to say is that there is no reason why André Breton should say of Césaire, 'Here is a black man who handles the French language as no white man today can.' " [47]

The tendency to designate and identify a person as a "black" or "Negro" when the designation is not necessary carries over into newspaper and magazine reporting of crimes. There was no need for *Time* magazine (July 19, 1968) to designate the race of the individual concerned in the following *Time* report: "In New York City, slum dwellers were sent

skidding for cover when Bobby Rogers, 31, Negro superintendent of a grubby South Bronx tenement, sprayed the
street with bullets from a sawed-off .30 cal. semi-automatic
carbine, killing three men and wounding a fourth." *Time*,
for whatever reason, identified the race of the person involved in this instance, but the reports on other criminal
offenses cited by *Time* on the same page did not indicate the
race of the "suspects." As a label of primary potency, "Negro" stands out over "superintendent."

The assumption that whites can understand and sympathize
with the blacks' dismay when black "suspects" are identified
by race and white "suspects" are not is apparently an un-
warranted assumption; or it may be possible that whites *do*
understand the dismay and precisely for that reason continue to designate the race of the black criminal suspect.

To argue that if the race is not mentioned in the news story
then the reader can assume that the suspect is white is not
acceptable for it makes all the difference if the suspect is
identified as "a Negro superintendent," "a white superintendent," or "a superintendent."

If, let's say we were told, day in and day out, that "a *white*
bank teller embezzled" or "a *white* service station operator
stole" or "a *white* unemployed laborer attacked," it would
make a difference in the same sense that it makes a difference
to identify the suspect as "Negro" or "black." If white suspects or criminals were always identified in the newspapers
and magazines as "a Caucasian gunman" or "a white rapist"
the effect would be for the reading public to wonder at such a
large number of whites committing crimes. But when whites
are criminally involved the practice is for the media not to
indicate the race and the result is that it becomes irrelevant; we become conscious that there was a gunman or a
rapist, but their being white is ignored. Just as soon as

blacks are identified by race it becomes very relevant and the result is: "Always reading about them blacks committing crimes. What can you expect?"

If many blacks find it hard to understand why whites have to designate a great writer or a great artist or a common criminal as "colored" or "Negro," so too do many blacks find it difficult to understand why whites must designate a black woman as a "Negress." Offensive as "Negress" is to most blacks, many whites still insist on using the term. In a July 28, 1968 *New York Times Magazine* article, the writer, discussing the campaigning of Nelson Rockefeller and Richard Nixon, wrote: "A fat Negress on the street says, passionately, 'Rocky! Rocky'!" As Gordon Allport has written in *The Nature of Prejudice,* "members of minority groups are often understandably sensitive to names given them. Not only do they object to deliberately insulting epithets, but sometimes see evil intent where none exists." [48] Allport gives two examples to make his point: one is the spelling of the word "Negro" with a small "n" and the other is the word "Negress." "Sex differentiations are objectionable," writes Allport, "since they seem doubly to emphasize differences: why speak of Jewess and not of Protestantess, or of Negress, and not of whiteness?" [49] Just as "Jewess" is offensive to the Jews, so too is "Negress" offensive to blacks. "A Negro woman" does not carry the same connotations as "Negress," the latter conveying an emotional emphasis on both the color and the sex of the individual. *Webster's New World Dictionary of the American Language* says of "Negress": "A Negro woman or girl: often a patronizing or contemptuous term."

The whites must make a serious conscious effort to discard the racist clichès of the past, the overt and covert language of racism. "Free, white, and 21" or "That's white of you" are phrases whites can no longer indulge in. Asking white Americans to change their language, to give up some of their clichès, is disturbing enough since the request implies a deficiency in the past use of that language; asking that they discard the language of racism is also disturbing because the people being asked to make the change, in effect, are being told that they had been the perpetrators and perpetuators of racism. Finally, and most important, calling the black American "nigger" or "boy," or "speaking down" to the Negro has given Whitey a linguistic power over the victimized blacks, a power many whites are unwilling or afraid to give up. A person's language is an extension of himself or herself and to attack that language is to attack the person. Difficult and painful as it may be for whites to discard their racist terms, phrases, and clichès, it must be done before blacks and whites can sit down to discuss seriously the eradication of white racism.

While the legislatures and courts have moved away from using phrases such as "inferior races," "racial pride," "racial integrity," and "mongrel breed of citizens," the language of white racism persists. And as long as it persists, as long as language is used to define a people as inferiors and nonpersons, the potential to do massive violence against those so defined is everpresent. In a speech delivered July 21, 1967, Floyd McKissick of the Congress of Racial Equality, warned:

"Yes — the Man has the capacity to neglect, to destroy, to shoot, to kill — if his victim is not white. He has the capacity for genocide. . . .

"No, genocide is not a simple matter. It cannot just happen. One group of people cannot just go ahead and wipe out another group of people. They must first pass through several stages — they must live out a peculiar and deadly pattern.

"The first prerequisite for a nation capable of genocide is the belief that they are superior to their victims. They must believe that they are entitled to the control of the life and death of their victims. . . .

"In America, as we have seen, the belief in white superiority runs deep. It was a dominant factor in the slave trade. The Black African wasn't recognized as a human being.

"A belief ferocious enough to allow human slavery cannot be dissipated by a mere century and, in America, it has been quietly reinforced." [50]

4

THE LANGUAGE OF INDIAN DERISION

Few white Americans of the past few centuries were as understanding as Benjamin Franklin when he said of the Indians in 1784: "Savages we call them because their manners differ from ours, which we think the perfection of civility, they think the same of theirs.... Our laborious manner of life, compared with theirs, they esteem slavish and base; and the learning on which we value ourselves, they regard as frivolous and useless." [1]

Still fewer whites ever recognized what Thomas Jefferson saw in the Indians: "I am safe in affirming that the proofs of genius given by the Indians of North America place them on a level with whites in the same uncultivated state. The North of Europe furnishes subjects enough for comparison with them, and for a proof of their equality, I have seen some thousands myself, and conversed much with them, and have found in them a masculine, sound understanding.... I believe the Indian to be body and mind equal to the white man." [2]

Had these images, these definitions prevailed, the oppression of Indians would have been much more difficult to justify. It was much more defensible to rob them of their lands, to deny them ordinary human rights and privileges by defining them as the Pueblo Indians were by the New Mexico Supreme Court in 1869: "They were wandering savages, given to murder, robbery, and theft, living on the game of the mountains, the forest, and the plains, unaccustomed to the cultivation of the soil, and unwilling to follow the pursuits of civilized man. Providence made this world for the use of the man who had the energy and industry to pull off his coat, and roll up his sleeves, and go to work on the land, cut down the trees, grub up the brush and briars, and stay there on it and work it for the support of himself and family, and a kind and thoughtful Providence did not charge man a single cent for the whole world made for mankind and intended for their benefit. Did the Indians ever purchase the land, or pay anyone a single cent for it? Have they any deed or patent on it, or has it been devised to them by anyone as their exclusive inheritance?

"Land was intended and designed by Providence for the use of mankind, and the game that it produced was intended for those too lazy and indolent to cultivate the soil. . .The idea that a handful of wild, half-naked, thieving, plundering, murdering savages should be dignified with the sovereign attributes of nations, enter into solemn treaties, and claim a country five hundred miles wide by one thousand miles long as theirs in fee simple, because they hunted buffalo and antelope over it, might do for beautiful reading in Cooper's novels or Longfellow's *Hiawatha*, but is unsuited to the intelligence and justice of this age, or the natural rights of mankind." [3]

As Peter Farb declared in the December 16, 1971 issue of *The New York Review*: "Cannibalism, torture, scalping, mutilation, adultery, incest, sodomy, rape, filth, drunkenness — such a catalogue of accusations against a people is an indication not so much of their depravity as that their land is up for grabs." [4]

The land-grabbing, the "de-civilization," the dehumanization and redefinition of the "American Indian" began with the arrival of Columbus in the New World. The various and diverse peoples of the "Americas," even though the differences between them were as great as between Italians and

Irish or Finns and Portuguese, were all dubbed "Indians," and then "American Indians." Having redefined the inhabitants, the invaders then proceeded to enslave, torture, and kill them, justifying this by labeling the Indians as "savages" and "barbarians."

Plundering and killing of the Indians in the West Indies outraged the Spanish Dominican missionary, Bartolome de las Casas, who provided the following account of the conquest of the Arawaks and Caribs in his *Brief Relation of the Destruction of the Indies:* "They [the Spaniards] came with their Horsemen well armed with Sword and Launce, making most cruel havocks and slaughters. . . . Overrunning Cities and Villages, where they spared no sex nor age; neither would their cruelty pity Women with childe, whose bellies they would rip up, taking the Infant to hew it in pieces. . . . The children they would take by the feet and dash their innocent heads against the rocks, and when they were fallen into the water, with a strange and cruel derision they would call to them to swim. . . . They erected certain Gallowses. . . upon every one of which they would hang thirteen persons, blasphemously affirming that they did it in honor of our Redeemer and his Apostles, and then putting fire under them, they burnt the poor wretches alive. Those whom their pity did think to spare, they would send away with their hands cut off, and so hanging by the skin." [5]

After the arrival of the Spaniards "whole Arawak villages disappeared through slavery, disease, and warfare, as well as by flight into the mountains. As a result the native population of Haiti, for example, declined from an estimated 200,000 in 1492 to a mere 29,000 only twenty-two years later." [6]

The ideas of white supremacy which the Europeans brought with them affected the redefinition of the Indians. In his book *The Indian Heritage in America*, Alvin M. Josephy, Jr. observes that "in the early years of the sixteenth century educated whites, steeped in the theological teaching of Europe, argued learnedly about whether or not Indians were humans with souls, whether they, too, derived from Adam and Eve (and were therefore sinful like the rest of mankind), or whether they were a previously subhuman species." [7] Uncivilized and satanic as the Indians may have been, according to the European invaders, they could be saved; but if they could not be saved then they would be destroyed.

As Roy H. Pearce has pointed out, "convinced thus of his divine right to Indian lands, the Puritan discovered in the Indians. . .evidence of a Satanic opposition to the very principle of divinity," [8] although, somehow, the Indian "also was a man who had to be brought to the civilized responsibilities of Christian manhood, a wild man to be improved along with wild lands, a creature who had to be made into a Puritan if he was to be saved. Save him, and you saved one of Satan's victims. Destroy him, and you destroyed one of Satan's partisans." [9] Indians who resisted Puritan intrusions of their lands were "heathens" who could be justifiably killed if they refused to give up their lands to the white invaders: "When the Pequots resisted the migration of settlers into the Connecticut Valley in 1637, a party of Puritans surrounded the Pequot village and set fire to it. . . . Cotton Mather was grateful to the Lord that 'on this day we have sent six hundred heathen souls to hell.' " [10]

The Europeans, having defined themselves as culturally superior to the inhabitants they found in the New World, proceeded to their "manifest destiny" through massive killing of the "savages." The "sense of superiority over the Indians which was fostered by the religious ideology they

carried to the new land," L. L. Knowles and K. Prewitt tell
us in *Institutional Racism in America*, "found its expression
in the self-proclaimed mission to civilize and Christianize —
a mission which was to find its ultimate expression in ideas
of a 'manifest destiny' and a 'white man's burden.' " [11] But
the Christianizing and "civilizing" process did not succeed
and "thus began an extended process of genocide, giving rise
to such aphorisms as 'The only good Indian is a dead Indian.'. . .Since Indians were capable of reaching only the
state of 'savage,' they should not be allowed to impede the
forward (westward, to be exact) progress of white civilization. The Church quickly acquiesced in this redefinition of
the situation." [12]

If the Indians were not defined as outright "savages" or
"barbarians," they were labeled "natives," and as Arnold
Toynbee has shrewdly observed in *A Study of History*, "when
we Westerners call people 'Natives' we implicitly take the
cultural colour out of our preceptions of them. We see
them as trees walking, or as wild animals infesting the country in which we happen to come across them. In fact, we see
them as part of the local flora and fauna, and not as men of
like passions with ourselves; and, seeing them thus as something infra-human, we feel entitled to treat them as though
they did not possess ordinary human rights." [13] Once the Indians were labeled "natives," their domestication or extermination became, ostensibly, permissible.

At the nation's Constitutional Convention in 1787 it had
to be decided which inhabitants of the total population in the
newly formed United States should be counted in determining
how many representatives each state would have in Congress.
The decision was that "representatives and direct taxes shall
be apportioned among the several states. . .according to their
respective numbers, which shall be determined by adding to

the whole number of free persons, including those bound to service for a term of ten years, and excluding Indians not taxed, three fifths of all other persons." The enslaved black came out three fifths of a person and the Indian was treated as a nonentity.

When the Indians had been defined as "savages" with no future, the final result, as Pearce states, "was an image of the Indian out of society and out of history." Once the Indians were successfully defined as governmental nonentities, no more justification was needed to drive them off their lands and to force them into migration and eventual death. During the nineteenth century, even "civilized Indians" found themselves being systematically deprived of life and property. The Five Civilized Tribes (Choctaws, Chicasaws, Creeks, Cherokees, and Seminoles) took on many of the characteristics of the whites' civilization: "Many of them raised stock, tilled large farms, built European style homes, and even owned Negro slaves like their white neighbors. They dressed like white men, learned the whites' methods, skills, and art, started small industries, and became Christians." [14]

They were still Indians, however, and in the 1820's and 1830's the United States Government forced the Five Civilized Tribes from their lands and homes and sent them "to new homes west of the Mississippi River to present-day Oklahoma, which was then thought to be uninhabitable by white men. Their emigrations were cruel and bitter trials." [15] Fifteen thousand Cherokees who had become "civilized" and "Christianized" and who resisted the whites' demands that they move west were systematically decimated by the United States Army: "Squads of soldiers descended upon isolated Cherokee farms and at bayonet point marched the families off to what today would be known as concentration camps. Torn from their homes with all the dispatch and efficiency

the Nazis displayed under similar circumstances, the families
had no time to prepare for the arduous trip ahead of them.
No way existed for the Cherokee family to sell its property
and possessions and the local Whites fell upon the lands,
looting, burning, and finally taking possession." [16]

In a speech he delivered in 1846 Senator Thomas Hart
Benton of Missouri spoke to the United States Senate about
the inferiority of the Indians and the superiority of the white
race. He gave the Indians a choice: become "civilized" or
face extinction. But as indicated above, the Indians' adoption
of the whites' civilization was no guarantee against suppression, cruelty, and extinction. Senator Benton expressed his
preference for the white "civilization" over the Indians'
"savagery": "The Red race has disappeared from the Atlantic Coast: the tribes that resisted civilization, met extinction. For my part, I cannot murmur at which seems to be
the effect of divine law. . . . Civilization, or extinction, has
been the fate of all people who have found themselves in the
track of the advancing Whites, and civilization, always the
preference of the Whites, has been pressed as an object,
while extinction has followed as a consequence of resistance.
The Black and Red Races have often felt their ameliorating
influence." [17]

During debate on peace with the Indians, Senator Abraham
Howard declared on July 17, 1867 that the Indian could
not be "civilized" or "Christianized": "The Indians are a
roving race. You will find it utterly impossible by any
course of education or teaching or preaching, or by whatever means you may see fit to employ, to reconcile the wild
Indians such as these tribes are to the business of agriculture
or to the habits of civilized life. That experiment has been
going on for the last two hundred years and more. It commenced with the very discovery of this country, and good

men, philanthropists, Christians, missionaries of every de-
nomination, have had the subject very much at heart, and
have expended millions of dollars from the days that Elliot
first commenced the attempt in Massachusetts down to the
present time; and what is the present result of all these
humane and philanthropic efforts to civilize and Christianize
the Indian? Sir, the net result of the whole is hardly worth
speaking about. From some fatality or other, no matter
what, it is perfectly apparent that the North American Indian
cannot be civilized, cannot be Christianized." [18]

Senator Howard went on to turn his attention to the necessity of the Indian to "yield before the advance of the white
man": "He cannot throw himself across the path of progress. It is the very nature of things that barbarism, which is
but another name for feebleness and dependence, must yield
before the firm tread of the white man, carrying forward, as
he always will, the flag and the institutions of civilization." [19]

Senator Howard's portrayal of the Indian as a "barbarian"
who could never be "civilized" was attacked by Senator
Edward Morrill in the Senate debate: "Sir, there are
civilized Indians in this country. Does the Senator know
that? There are many civilized Indians. In spite of the
merciless and faithless policy of this Government there are
civilized Indians, and they are many of them, and there are
enough to repel this assumption of the honorable Senator
and to vindicate their race to a place in the scale of humanity,
and show that they are the children of a common father;
that they belong to human kind, that they are susceptible to
its emotions, that they may be influenced by the considera-
tions which influence other human beings. The history of
American civilization shows no such thing as the honorable
Senator supposes, and I am sorry that the utterance has come
from him." [20]

Later in the debate, Senator Morrill spoke of the spirit in which Indians were absorbed into white communities: "Is the spirit of the border eminently kind to the Indian? Not a bit of it. The sentiment is, 'he is a savage; he is a barbarian; a bounty on his head; is his presence compatible with our rights?' That is the spirit of the border. Nobody will deny that. And that spirit is to absorb him! I have already said what that means; it means extinction. Absorption is the Indian's scalp for a bounty." [21]

In response to Morrill's criticisms of the whites' treatment of the Indians, Senator Howard retorted: "Sir, it is not necessary for me to vindicate the character and policy of the Government of the United States against so serious an imputation as this; and I will content myself simply saying that, according to my reading of the history of our relations with the Indians, there are very few cases in which the United States have been in the wrong." [22] Having defined the Indians as he did, Senator Howard's attempts to justify the whites' treatment of the Indians was greatly simplified.

In 1879, with the addition of the Fourteenth Amendment to the Constitution, it was decided that "all persons born or naturalized in the United States, and subject to the jurisdiction thereof, are citizens of the United States and of the State wherein they reside."

But the Fourteenth Amendment was subsequently held not to apply to the Indians. The question came to the United States Supreme Court in 1884 in *Elk v. Wilkins*,[23] a case involving an Indian who had moved off the reservation, severed tribal ties and completely surrendered himself to the jurisdiction of the United States and of his resident state, where he attempted to register to vote and was refused. The Court decided against John Elk, contending that the Fourteenth Amendment had not made him a citizen. In its decision the

Court affirmed that the Fourteenth Amendment applied to the freed slaves, "but Indians not taxed are still excluded from the count, for the reason that they are not citizens. Their absolute exclusion from the basis of representation, in which all other persons are now included, is wholly inconsistent with their being considered citizens." [24] The Court placed the "privilege" of defining citizenship rights of Indians in the hands of the national government; it was the government which was to decide whether the Indians had advanced far enough into the white civilization to warrant citizenship. Even the Indians who had left their tribes to take up the ways of the whites, who left their "barbaric" state to become "civilized," could in no way be defined as citizens.

In *Elk v. Wilkins* the Court cited Judge Deady of Oregon, who stated in *United States v. Osborne* that "an Indian cannot make himself a citizen of the United States without the consent and co-operation of the government. The fact that he has abandoned his nomadic life or tribal relations, and adopted the habits and manners of civilized people, may be a good reason why he should be made a citizen of the United States, but does not of itself make him one." [25] By some strange white logic, the blacks taken from their tribal homes in Africa to be placed in slavery in the United States came to be defined as citizens of this country, while the original inhabitants, the Indians, were to remain defined as inferior and uncivilized nomads in their own land.

In an effort to "civilize" the Indians, the Government established schools for the "savages," and one aspect of the education received by the children was an attempt to teach the Indians to pay homage to their oppressor. In 1901 the United States Superintendent of Indian Schools prepared "A Course of Study for Indian Schools" which was printed by the Government Printing Office and distributed to "Agents, Superintendents, and Teachers of Schools." It was the author's hope that this course of study would lead the Indians to "better morals, a more patriotic and Christian citizenship and ability for self support." [26] While most of the publication dealt with subjects such as agriculture, baking, basketry, gardening, and harness making, a chapter was devoted to the study of history. While recognizing the need for the teacher to relate to the Indians something about their heritage, the chapter also suggested that the teacher instruct the youths in the history of the United States; the course of study recommended that the Indians should know enough about United States history "to be good, patriotic citizens:"

"They should learn a few important dates, such as that of the discovery of America, settlement of Virginia, Declaration of Independence, etc.

"Describe historical events, as the discovery of America and the landing of the Pilgrims.

"See that the event turns on the person, showing examples of patriotism, valor, self-sacrifice, heroism. . . .

"The names of our greatest men, such as Washington, Franklin, and Lincoln, should also be learned and something about the character and work of each.'" [37]

The chapter suggested that the teacher also adapt "stories appropriate to Thanksgiving, Christmas, New Year's Day, Arbor Day, etc. Enlarge upon national holidays; history of our flag; patriotism; loyalty to a cause; one's institution; one's country." [38]

The teacher was told that "patriotic songs must be taught in every school, and every child should be familiar with the words as well as the music of our inspiring national songs." [29] Further, "in every school the salute to the flag must be taught and where the climate will permit, this exercise must be engaged in out of doors, by the whole school, morning and evening; and where the climate is too severe, it can be done in the classroom daily and at the evening hour." [30] This practice of demanding that the oppressed honor and pay homage to the oppressor was itself part of the dehumanizing process.

By some strange reasoning, "the important date" of the settlement of Virginia was considered something which would contribute to the "patriotism" of the Indians, although in Virginia the white invaders had referred to the Indians as "beasts," "savages," "miscreants," and "barbarians." In Virginia in 1622, after the Indians had killed approximately three hundred fifty English invaders, the English took revenge by burning the crops of the Indians, putting the torch to their homes, and driving them from their villages. In 1623 Indians who approached the Virginians with the intent to sue for peace were shot. To teach Indian youths to see the white Virginia "colonists" as examples of "patriotism, valor, self-sacrifice, and heroism," to teach these students to regard the very people who had suppressed and killed their ancestors as exemplary was a travesty of education.

The travesty and humiliation were compounded by requiring the Indian children to learn the words of "our inspiring national songs." The significance to the Indian of one of these songs has been observed by Vine Deloria, Jr., in *Custer Died for Your Sins: An Indian Manifesto:* "One day at a conference we were singing 'My Country 'Tis of Thee' and we came across the part that goes: 'Land where our father died, Land of the Pilgrims' pride. . . .' Some of us broke out laughing when we realized that our fathers undoubtedly died trying to keep those Pilgrims from stealing our land. In fact, many of our fathers died because the Pilgrims killed them as witches. We didn't feel much kinship with those Pilgrims, regardless of who they did in." [31]

Not only were Indian youths to be taught to show delight in the discovery of America and the settlement of Virginia and to learn the words of "our inspiring national songs," they were also to be taught the salute to the flag of the United States at a time when Indian citizenship was not guaranteed, when Indian suffrage was denied in various states, when "liberty and justice for all" simply did not apply to Indians. The children were in effect forced to salute the flag under which their conquerors and oppressors had marched. One might as well have forced the blacks in this country to salute the Confederate flag or the Jews in Germany to salute the Nazi swastika flag. If an oppressed group of people can be forced, without their actively rebelling, to pledge allegiance to the flag of their masters, the humiliation and subjugation are outwardly manifested for all to see.

One of the rituals some Indians were subjected to when they sought to become citizens required they give up their "Indian names" and take on "white ones." The ritual clearly compelled the Indian to deny his or her previous identity through the renaming and redefining process. For male Indians the procedure was as follows:

"For men: (Read name) — (White name). What was your Indian name? (Gives name). — (Indian name.) I hand you a bow and an arrow. Take this bow and shoot the arrow. (He shoots.)

— (Indian name.) You have shot your last arrow. That means that you are no longer to live the life of an Indian. You are from this day forward to live the life of the white man. . . ." [32]

The male Indian then was asked to place his hands on a plow to symbolize the choice to "live the life of the white man — and the white man lives by work." Then he was given a purse: "(White name.) I give you a purse. This purse will always say to you that the money you gain from your labor must be wisely kept." Then an American flag was placed in his hands and he was told: "This is the only flag you have ever had or ever will have. . . ." The ritual was similar for the female Indian, except that she had placed into her hands a work bag and a purse. In taking these items she had "chosen the life of the white woman — and the white woman loves her home." [33] A ritualistic effort requiring one to deny one's identity, to give up one's control over his or her self, could hardly have been more complete.

While the state and church as institutions have defined the Indian into subjugation, there has been in operation the use of a suppressive language by society at large which has perpetuated the dehumanization of the Indian. Commonly used words and phrases relegate the Indian to an inferior, infantile status: "The only good Indian is a dead Indian"; "Give it back to the Indians"; "drunken Indians"; "dumb Indians"; "Redskins"; "Indian giver." Writings and speeches include references to the "Indian Problem" in the same manner that references have been made by whites to "the Negro problem" and by the Nazis to "the Jewish problem." There was no "Jewish problem" in Germany until the Nazis linguistically created the myth; there was no "Negro problem" until white Americans created the myth; similarly, the "Indian problem" has been created in such a way that the oppressed, not the oppressor, evolve as "the problem."

As the list of negative "racial characteristics" of the

"Indian race" grew over the years, the redefinition of the individual Indian became easier and easier. He or she was trapped by the racial definitions, stereotypes, and myths. No matter how intelligent, how "civilized" the Indian became, he or she was still an Indian. Even the one who managed to become a citizen (prior to 1924) could not discard his or her 'Indian-ness' sufficiently to participate fully in white society. The law's language was used to reinforce the redefinition of the oppressed into nonpersons and this language of suppression, as law, became governmentally institutionalized, and in effect legitimatized. In 1831, the United States Supreme Court defined the Indians "in a state of pupilage. Their relation to the United States resembles that of a ward to his guardian." [34]

In 1832 the Alabama Supreme Court labeled the Indians "beasts," "savages," and "wildmen," definitions which in turn were used to "prove" that the Indians were not entitled to "rank in the family of independent nations," that the Indians' lands could be appropriated by the whites since "the right of the agriculturists was paramount to that of the hunter tribes." [35]

Alabama's high court asked: "Were the natives of this vast continent, at the period of the advent of the first Europeans, in the possession and enjoyment of those attributes of sovereignty, to entitle them to rank in the family of independent governments?" [36] The court answered its question by declaring in part: "The fairest quarter of the globe is roamed over by the wildman, who has no permanent abiding place, but moves from camp to camp, as the pursuit of game may lead him. He knows not the value of any of the comforts of civilized life. As well might a treaty, on terms of equality, be attempted with the beast of the same forest that he inhabits." [37]

In 1857, at the same time he was denying human rights to the black slaves in the United States, Chief Justice Taney of the United States Supreme Court declared in his *Dred Scott* opinion: "Congress might...have authorized the naturalization of Indians, because they were aliens and foreigners. But, in their then untutored and savage state, no one would have thought of admitting them as citizens in a civilized community.... No one supposed then that any Indian would ask for, or was capable of enjoying, the privileges of an American citizen, and the word white was not used with any particular reference to them." [38]

One of the most blatant examples of the use of the racial characteristic argument is evident in an 1897 Minnesota Supreme Court decision dealing with the indictment of one Edward Wise for selling intoxicating liquors to an Indian who had severed all his relations with his tribe and had through the provision of the "Land in Severality Act" of February 8, 1887, become a citizen of the United States. Wise was indicted for violating a statute which provided that "whosoever sells...any spiritous liquors or wines to any Indian in this state shall on conviction thereof be punished...."

In finding against Wise, the Minnesota Supreme Court emphasized the weakness of the "Indian race" and the fact that as a race Indians were not as "civilized" as the whites: "...in view of the nature and manifest purpose of this statute and the well-known conditions which induce its enactment, there is no warrant for limiting it by excluding from its operation sales of intoxicating liquors to any person of Indian blood, even although he may have become a citizen of the United States, by compliance with the act of congress. The statute is a police regulation. It was enacted in view of the well-known social condition, habits, and tendencies of

Indians as a race. While there are doubtless notable individual exceptions to the rule, yet it is a well-known fact that Indians as a race are not as highly civilized as the whites; that they are less subject to moral restraint, more liable to acquire an inordinate appetite for intoxicating liquors, and also more liable to be dangerous to themselves and others when intoxicated." [39]

The Minnesota statute, said the court, applied to and included "all Indians as a race, without reference to their political status. . . . The difference in condition between Indians as a race and the white race constituted a sufficient basis of classification." [40] Under the court's reasoning, the individual Indian could not control his or her identity. Like it or not, the individual Indian was defined by the court's language, by the "well-known fact" that "Indians as a race are not as highly civilized as whites," that Indians are "less subject to moral restraint." Like it or not, the individual Indian was identified in terms of "characteristics" of the "Indians as a race," whether he or she had those characteristics or not, whether he or she was a citizen of the United States or not.

Twenty years later Minnesota denied voting rights to Indians on the basis of their not being "civilized." In *In re Liquor Election in Beltrami County*,[41] the state's Supreme Court, denying voting rights to the Minnesota Indians involved in that 1917 case, noted their "uncivilized" status. The court's language was in keeping with the spirit of the Minnesota Constitution which stipulated that every male person of the age of twenty-one years and older belonging to one of the following three classes was entitled to vote if he had resided in the state and election district the specified time: (1) citizens of the United States who have been such for a period of three months next preceding any election;

(2) persons of mixed Indian blood, who have adopted customs and habits of civilization; (3) persons of Indian blood who have adopted the language, customs, and habits of civilization.

The inhumanity of the racist language in *In re Liquor Election in Beltrami County* was complemented by the sexism in the decision: "It is true that a mixed-blood Indian is a citizen if his father was.... And no doubt more mixed bloods spring from a white father and an Indian or mixed-blood mother than from a white mother and an Indian or mixed-blood father. But it is also probably true that very many of the mixed bloods of a white father are not the issue of lawful wedlock. An illegitimate child takes the status of the mother.... It is also well known that many of the white men who assumed relations with Indian women were not citizens. The citizenship of mixed and full bloods residing upon this reservation seems to us so extremely doubtful that we think contestant made a prima facie case of non-citizenship as to all of the 68 who voted...." [42]

Minnesota's Supreme Court then turned its attention to whether the Indians in question were qualified to vote under the second provision cited above. It decided that the mixed-bloods did not fall into the second category: "It is not to be denied that these mixed-bloods have adopted the habits and customs of civilization to a certain extent. With the assistance of the federal government and the schools maintained by it these Indians have advanced considerable on the road to civilization. They, however, still cling to some of the customs and habits of their race, and are governed in their relation with each other by their peculiar tribal rules and practices." [48]

Asserting that the framers of the Constitution did not intend to grant the right of suffrage to persons who were under no obligation to obey the laws enacted as a result of such grant, the court said: "No one should participate in the making of laws which he need not obey. As truly said by contestant: 'The tribal Indian contributes nothing to the state. His property is not subject to taxation, or to the process of its courts. He bears none of the burdens of civilization and performs none of the duties of the citizens." [44] The court concluded by stating that the right of suffrage in Minnesota was "held out as an inducement to the Indians to sever their tribal relations and adopt in all respects the habits and customs of civilization." [45]

How was an Indian to demonstrate that he or she had taken on "the habits and customs of civilization"? How was a person of mixed-blood to demonstrate that he or she was living "a civilized life"? In a case involving the segregated schools in Sitka, Alaska, the court dealt with a statute which said in part: "That the schools specified and provided for in this act shall be devoted to the education of white children and children of mixed blood who lead a civilized life. The education of the Eskimos and Indians in the district of Alaska shall remain under the direction and control of the Secretary of the Interior...." The court explained, "a clear distinction is here made between the school for the native — i.e., the Eskimo and the Indian, whether civilized or otherwise — and the school for the white child, or the child with the white man's blood in its veins, though it be mixed with that of another race. But of the child of mixed blood there is made the further requirement, to wit, that he shall live in a civilized life." [46]

In deciding that two of the children, ages seven and eight, had been legitimately prohibited from attending the whites' school, the court pointed to the "fact" that the children came from a family which was not "civilized": "Walton [stepfather of the youths] owns a house in the native village, lying on the outskirts of the town of Sitka. The children live there with their mother and stepfather. Their associates and play-mates are presumably the native children who live in the Indian village. So far as these plaintiffs are concerned, there is nothing to indicate any difference between them and the other children of the Sitka native village, except the testi-mony of Walton and others as to Walton's business. Walton conducts a store on the edge of the town of Sitka, in which he manufacturers and sells Indian curios, and for which he pays the business license tax by the laws of Alaska. . . . He and his family have adopted the white man's style of dress. All who testified concerning Walton himself speak of him as an industrious, law-abiding, intelligent native. He seems, so far as business matters are concerned, to have endeavored to conduct his business according to civilized methods, even to the installation of an expensive cash register in his store. He speaks, reads, and writes the English language." [47]

But conducting business, manufacturing curios, paying the business license tax, adopting the whites' style of dress, being industrious, law-abiding, and intelligent "native," speaking, reading and writing English — characteristics and qualities many whites themselves did not possess —were not enough to make the Walton family "civilized."

The court went on to ask: "What is the manner of their life? What are their domestic habits? Who are their asso-ciates and intimates? These matters do not appear. True, the Waltons are members of the Presbyterian Church; but many natives, for whom the claim of civilization would not be made, are members of churches of the various denominations which are striving to better the conditions of this country. . . . The burden of establishing that the plaintiffs live the civilized life is upon them, and I fail to find in the testimony evidence of a condition that inclines me to the opinion that the...children have that requisite." [48] Having thus defined the "native" family and children the court justified the segregation of the children and ordered them out of the whites' school.

In determining the "civilized" status of another family whose child was also prohibited from attending the white school the court took into consideration the following:

"It appears that his [plaintiff's] wife is a good house-keeper, so far as their means, and station in life will allow her to be; that the pots and kettles and frying pans are not left upon the floor, after the native fashion, but are hung up, and that curtains drape the windows of their house. This indicates progress; but does it satisfy the test? It is urged that Allard and his wife have been entertained by white men of culture and refinement; but that cannot be considered as a criterion of civilization...it is an evidence of the kindliness and of the interest and effort of the hosts in behalf of a people among and for whom they have labored long and assiduously, not an evidence of the civilization of the guests.... Those who from choice make their homes among an uncivilized or semi-civilized people and find there their sole social enjoyments and personal pleasures and associations cannot, in my opinion, be classed with those who live a civilized life." [49] As in the Walton case, the court found the Allard children and family "uncivilized" and denied the children access to the Sitka school established for "the education of white children and children of mixed blood who lead a civilized life."

In 1944 five states prohibited intermarriages between Indians and whites: Arizona, Nevada, North Carolina, South Carolina, and Virginia. The Supreme Court of Arizona upheld a lower court holding that the marriage between a descendant of an Indian and a member of the Caucasian race was illegal and void. Arizona's miscegenation statute read: "The marriage of persons of Caucasian blood, or their descendants, with Negroes, Hindus, Mongolians, members of the Malay race, or Indians, and their descendants, shall be null and void." In describing the two persons involved in the marriage considered in *State v. Pass*, the court stated:

"The evidence is undisputed that defendant's mother was the child of an English father and Piute Indian woman and that his father was a Mexican, so he was a descendant of three races, to wit, Caucasian, Indian and Mexican.

"Ruby Contreras Pass testified that her father was a Spaniard and her mother half French and half Mexican. And to the question, 'Do you have any Indian blood in you?' she answered, 'Not that I know of.' Thus she is a descendant of two races, to wit, Spanish and French." [50]

The absurdity of Arizona's miscegenation statute was not missed by the court even though it held the statute constitutional: "It makes a marriage of a person of Caucasian blood and his descendants to one of Indian blood and his descendants null and void. Under it a descendant of mixed blood such as defendant cannot marry a Caucasian or a part Caucasian, for the reason that he is part Indian. He cannot marry an Indian or a part Indian because he is part Caucasian. For the same reason a descendant of mixed Negro and Caucasian blood may not contract marriage with a Negro or a part Negro, etc. We think the language used by the lawmakers went far beyond what was intended. In trying to prevent the white race from interbreeding with Indians, Negroes, Mongolians, etc., it has made it unlawful for a person with 99% Indian blood and 1% Causasian blood to marry an Indian, or a person with 99% Caucasian blood and 1% Indian blood to marry a Caucasian. We mention this and the absurd situations it creates believing and hoping that the legislature will correct it by naming the percentage of Indian and other tabooed blood that will invalidate a marriage. The miscegenation statutes of the different states do fix the degree or percentage of blood in a Negro, an Indian, etc. preventing marriage alliances with Caucasians." [51]

In 1944, two years after the above Arizona Supreme Court decision, the Circuit Court of Appeals, Tenth Circuit, decided in Oklahoma that the marriage of Stella Sands, "a full-blooded Creek Indian," to William Stevens who was of African descent was a "nullity" since under Oklahoma law as "a full-blooded Creek Indian" she was classified as white, and Oklahoma law prohibited marriages between whites and persons of African descent. In deciding the marriage a "nullity," the Circuit Court cited Article XXIII, Section 11, of the Oklahoma Constitution which provided that "wherever in the constitution and laws of the state the word or words 'colored' or 'colored race,' 'negro' or 'negro race,' are used it or they shall be construed to mean and apply to all persons of African descent, and that the term 'white race' shall include all other persons." [52] The effect of the inconsistencies of white legislators and judges was that a person was defined "white" in one state and not "white" in another.

Arizona, the state with the largest Indian population, until 1948 did not allow Indians the right to vote. Article 7 of the state's Constitution concerning the qualifications of voters placed the Indians in the same category as traitors and felons, the same category as persons not of sound mind and the insane. Article 7 provided in part: "No person under guardianship, *non compos mentis* or insane shall be qualified to vote in any election or shall any person convicted of treason or felony, be qualified to vote at any election unless restored to civil rights."

In 1928 the Arizona Supreme Court decided in *Porter v. Hall*[53] that Arizona Indians did not have the right to vote since they were within the specific provisions of Article 7 denying suffrage to "persons under guardianship." The court held that "so long as the federal government insists that, notwithstanding their citizenship, their responsibility under our law differs from that of the ordinary citizen, and that they are, or may be, regulated by that government, by virtue of its guardianship, in any manner different from that which may be used in the regulation of white citizens, they are, within the meaning of our constitutional provision, 'persons under guardianship,' and not entitled to vote." [54]

In defining the Indians of Arizona as it did in *Porter v. Hall*, the Arizona Supreme Court denied suffrage rights to the Indians even though four years earlier, on June 2, 1924, all non-citizen Indians born within the territorial limits of the United States were declared citizens thereof by an Act of Congress. After devoting a paragraph to defining "insanity" and *"non compos mentis,"* the court followed with a definition and discussion of "persons under guardianship," the category into which the Indians were placed:

"Broadly speaking, persons under guardianship may be defined as those, who, because of some peculiarity of status, defect of age, understanding, or self-control, are considered incapable of managing their own affairs, and who therefore have some other person lawfully invested with the power and charged with the duty of taking care of their persons or managing their property, or both. It will be seen from the foregoing definitions that there is one common quality found in each: The person falling within any one of the classes is to some extent and for some reason considered by the law as incapable of managing his own affairs as a normal person, and needing some special care from the state." [55]

In 1948, however, the *Porter* decision was overruled in the case of *Harrison v. Laveen*,[56] thus allowing Indians in Arizona the right to vote. In the 1948 decision, the Supreme Court of Arizona stated that the designation of "persons under guardianship" as it appeared in Article 7 did not apply to Indians. As to the argument that the Indians generally fell into that group of people "incapable of managing their own affairs," the court said in 1948 that "to ascribe to all Indians residing on reservations the quality of being 'incapable of handling their own affairs in an ordinary manner' would be a grave injustice, for amongst them are educated persons as fully capable of handling their affairs as their white neighbors." [57]

At long last, four and a half centuries after Columbus "discovered" America, almost all the descendants of the original occupants of this land were allowed by the descendants of the invaders to participate through the vote, in affecting some control (however small) over their destiny in their own land. Almost all of the "red natives" of the land finally were recognized legally as beings as fully capable of handling their affairs as "their white neighbors." Almost all.

As late as the middle of the 1950's Indians were still battling for the right to vote. In 1956, the Utah Supreme Court, in *Allen v. Merrell*,[58] denied the vote to reservation Indians in Utah, arguing, among other things, that low literacy and lack of civic involvement and responsibilities were Indian characteristics which disqualified them from having voting rights in Utah. The Utah court listed the Indians' "deficiencies":

"It is not subject to dispute that Indians living on reservations are extremely limited in their contact with state government and its units and for this reason also, have much less in-

terest in or concern with it than do other citizens. It is a matter of common knowledge that all except a minimal percentage of reservation Indians live, not in communities, but
in individual dwellings or hogans remotely isolated from
others and from contact with the outside world. Though such
a state is certainly not without its favorable aspects, they
have practically no access to newspapers, telephones, radio
or television; a very high percentage of them are illiterate;
and they do not speak English but in their dealings with
others and even in their tribal courts, use only their native
Indian languages." [59]

But how to reconcile the fact that Utah had no literacy requirement for voters with the argument that, since the Indians were illiterate they could not be allowed to vote? The
Utah Supreme Court added the following footnote to its
"observation" about the high percentage of the Indians being
illiterate: "Utah has no literacy requirement. This observation relates only to their present general character of life." [60]
After pointing out the Indians' lack of civic involvement,
the court stated that "it is thus plain to be seen that in a
county where the Indian population would amount to a sub-
stantial proportion of the citizenry, or may even outnumber
the other inhabitants, allowing them to vote might place sub-
stantial control of the county government and expenditures
of its funds in a group of citizens who, as a class, had extremely limited interest in its function and very little responsibility in providing the financial support thereof." [61] In
effect the same legal system which made it virtually impossible for Indians to practice "civic involvement" ruled that
Indians could not vote because of their lack of "civic involvement." The same system which kept the Indians isolated
ruled that Indians could not vote because they lived in com-

munities and dwellings "isolated from others and from contact with the outside world."

The definitions and stereotypes of the Indians developed over the past three centuries found their way into the history books. The linguistic dehumanization of Indians in history texts and the effects of these portrayals on Indian children have been noted by Alvin Josephy, Jr., Mary Gloyne Byler and others.

Josephy, observing that "many historians termed them [Indians] dirty, lazy, brutish, unproductive, and on the level with wild beasts," [62] has called attention to the effects of such definitions: "There are now some 750,000 Indians and Eskimos in the United States, and many of their children are attending schools and colleges where they are subjected to the use of insulting books. Their high dropout rates, self-hatred, a suicide rate far in excess of the national average, and their lack of motivation can be traced in great part to the feelings of disgrace and humiliation they suffer from their continual confrontation with stereotype thinking about them." [63]

In her study of the image of American Indians projected by non-Indian writers, Mary Gloyne Byler observes that "it has been well established by sociologists and psychologists that the effect on children of negative stereotypes and derogatory images is to engender and perpetuate undemocratic and unhealthy attitudes that will plague our society for years to come." [64]

Once one has been categorized through the language of oppression, one loses most of the power to determine one's future and control over one's identity and destiny. As a writer observes in *Our Brother's Keeper: The Indian in White America*, "ultimately, self-realization requires the power to shape one's future, to control one's destiny, to choose from a variety of alternatives. The Indian has no such power, no control and no choice." [65] Once the Indians had been successfully defined by the Europeans and their descendants as "heathens," "beasts," "savages," "barbarians," "wildmen',' "uncivilized," "in a state of pupilage," their power to define themselves and their destinies passed from their own hands to the hands of their oppressors.

5

THE LANGUAGE OF SEXISM

While the language of racial and ethnic oppression is often blatant and relatively easy to identify, the language of sexism is more subtle and pervasive. Our everyday speech reflects the "superiority" of the male and the "inferiority" of the female, resulting in a master-subject relationship. The language of sexism relegates the woman to the status of children, servants, and idiots, to being the "second sex" and to virtual invisibility. The progress implied in the advertising slogan "You've come a long way, baby" notwithstanding, the language of sexism remains with us and exerts an influence on the male's attitudes towards and control over women and the women's attitudes toward themselves. More accurate than the above slogan is the feminist's response: "If I've come such a long way, how come you still call me baby?"

The need to eradicate the language of sexism to bring about equality of the sexes has been recognized by a variety of writers. Deborah Rosenfelt and Florence Howe have pointed out that "a number of reputable linguists believe that linguistic systems are partially determined by underlying metaphysical assumptions about the structure of reality. Linguists argue about the precise nature of the interaction between language, thought, and culture, but it seems clear that language as a form of social behavior does both reflect and help to perpetuate deeply held cultural attitudes. Among these attitudes — and this is an area that traditional linguists have hardly touched upon — are those concerning the relationships between men and women." [1] "By calling attention to sexist usage," continue Rosenfelt and Howe, "feminists hope to change not only the language — the surface behavior — but the underlying attitudes that determine and, in a constant interaction, are determined by the behavior." [2]

Jessica Murray has expressed much the same view: "Language is a powerful conceptual force, and, as a transmitter of society's deep biases, it can be a means of conditioning our thoughts. I think it has been amply demonstrated that words are not mere empty vessels of syntax and semantics: they can fairly overflow with implicit opinion, and they can and do perpetuate prejudice. . . . It is true that language only represents a phenomenon that is almost too vast to contemplate changing. But the role of language in perpetuating the archetype of women-as-an-extra-human could be changed, it seems to me, by adopting new language conventions." [3]

Our sexist language, according to Aileen Hernandez, past president of the National Organization for Women, makes it abundantly clear that "in all areas that really count, we discount women." Sexist language manifests itself in various ways:

" 'Mankind' is the generic term for all people or all males, but there is no similar dual meaning for 'womankind.' The masculine pronoun is used to refer to both men and women in general discussions.

"The Constitution of the United States is replete with sexist language — Senators and Representatives are 'he'; the President is obviously 'he' and even the fugitive from justice is 'he' in our Constitution. . . .

"But just in case we as women manage to escape the brainwashing that assigns us to 'our place' in the order of things, the language continues to get the message across.

"There is a 'housewife' but no 'househusband'; there's a 'housemother' but no 'housefather'; there's a 'kitchenmaid' but no 'kitchenman'; unmarried women cross the threshold from 'bachelor girl' to 'spinster' to 'old maid,' but unmarried men are 'bachelors' forever." [4]

Writing in *Women: A Journal of Liberation*, Emily Toth has observed that "generally, women lack their own words for professional positions: a woman must be a 'female judge,' 'female representative,' 'madam chairman,' or — a ghastly pun — a 'female mailman." [5] She notes that "one textbook defines Standard English as that language spoken by 'educated professional people and their wives.' " [6] She might have added the *Webster's New World Dictionary of the American Language* definition of "honorarium": "a payment to a professional man for services on which no fee is set or legally obtainable."

Alma Graham tells us in an article titled "The Making of a Nonsexist Dictionary" that "at every level of achievement and activity — from primitive man to the man of the hour — woman is not taken into account. Consider the congressman. He is a man of the people. To prove that he's the best man for the job, he takes his case to the man in the street. He is a champion of the workingman. He speaks for the little man. He has not forgotten the forgotten man. And he firmly believes: one man, one vote. Consider the policeman or fireman, the postman or milkman, the clergyman or businessman." [7] So ingrained is the language of sexism that it is with great effort and some resistance that people will refer to a "jurywoman," "chairwoman," "churchwoman," or "journeywoman." Instead, the females all end up "countrymen," "middlemen," "selectmen," "jurymen" when these groups are referred to generally.

Not only does the woman end up a "man," she also finds herself labeled "he" or "him" or "his" when the pronoun is used as a neuter to designate anyone, female or male.

Lynne T. White, former president of Mills College, has commented on this problem of women coming out male through the use of masculine pronouns: "The grammar of English dictates that when a referent is either of indeterminate sex or both sexes, it shall be considered masculine. The penetration of this habit of language into the minds of little girls as they grow up to be women is more profound than most people, including most women, have recognized: it implies that personality is really a male attribute, and that women are human subspecies. . . . It would be a miracle if a girl-baby, learning to use the symbols of our tongue, could escape some wound to her self-respect; whereas a boy-baby's ego is bolstered by the pattern of our language." [8]

In her study dealing with the response of individuals to the pronoun "he" Virginia Kidd found that "the use of the male pronoun as the generic is not generally interpreted as representative of a neutral antecedent; that in fact the antecedent is considered male; that this interpretation of the antecedent as male is stronger in cases where the societal stereotypes of the male role coincides with the pronoun is often strong enough to be indicated in cases where other traits of the antecedent are admittedly unknown." [9] Kidd concludes that the results of her study "seem eminently clear: use of the masculine pronoun as the generic simply does not accomplish the purpose for which it is intended. The masculine pronoun does not suffice as a verbal indicator in situations where persons of either sex could be the antecedent." [10]

Rosenfelt and Howe report that "at a summer workshop a Feminist Press staff member used a simple device to illustrate the feelings of invisibility that the 'universal' *he* can arouse in women. She substituted the feminine pronoun: 'the teacher. . .she.' Finally a principal (male) could take it no longer. 'Why are you doing that, Marj?' he asked plaintively; 'why do you keep saying *she?*' With all eyes on her, Marj responded pleasantly, without embarrassment, 'why, I'm using the word generically.' Then there was laughter, an explosive release of tension. But the point had been made, and as the workshop went on, the participants were careful to use either he/she or the plural. Perhaps *he* was not so generic after all?" [11]

The pervasiveness of linguistic male predominance is exemplified by the fact that the very women who are attempting to bring about the women's liberation sometimes have fallen into the trap of using sexist language. The feminist magazine *Aphra*, for example, gave its readers the following information about one of its contributors: "Bernice Abbott is to have a one-man show at the Museum of Modern Art this winter...." [12] On one occasion I heard a woman discussing child-adoption regulations, and she remarked to her audience that "the women at the adoption agency acted as middlemen."

Even the National Organization for Women has placed men in higher precedence. The first paragraph of its 1966 Statement of Purpose declares: "We, men and women who hereby constitute ourselves as the National Organization for women, believe the time has come for a new movement toward true equality for all women in America, and toward a fully equal partnership of the sexes, as part of the world-wide revolution of human rights now taking place within and beyond our national borders."

The firstness of men in "We, men and women...." reveals that the "liberated" women find it hard to shake off a part of the language of sexism. The statement, considering the context, should begin, "We, women and men...." The connotations of the two phrases are entirely different. The blacks of the 1960's recognized that "American Negro" was the white's definition which relegated black identity to a

secondary status. Why was it, the blacks asked, that everyone else was an "Italian-American," a "German-American,"
or an "Irish-American," but the blacks were always "American Negro?" (See chapter on the language of white racism.)
Just as the blacks began to insist on defining themselves and
bringing into question the firstness of their "masters," so too
will women have to use language more carefully to avoid
words and phrases which define them as the "second sex,"
even second temporally in sentences.

There are many occasions when "women and men" would
be more appropriate than "men and women." In fact, one
might argue that since women are a majority in this nation
we should henceforth always speak of "the women and men of
this nation" instead of "the men and women of this nation."
The firstness of the male has always appeared evident when
male and female names are put side by side: Jack and Jill,
Hansel and Gretel, Romeo and Juliet, Antony and Cleopatra,
Dick and Jane, John and Marsha. As for the firstness of the
female, there isn't much more than Snow White and the
Seven Dwarfs.

In the church we have the "clergyman," the "altar boy,"
the Father, Son, and the Holy Ghost. Males dominate in
Christianity not only in language, but also in terms of the
decision-making powers, a domination which can partly be
attributed to the language of sexism. This male domination
exists despite the fact that "every survey that measures sex
differences in religiosity shows that females attend church
more frequently than males, pray more often, hold firmer
beliefs, cooperate more in church programs. This is true at
all age levels from childhood to senior-citizen, and of both
single and married women, of women gainfully employed
and home-makers." [13] But what is a woman to do when in
Scriptures she is told: "Wives, submit yourselves unto your

own husbands, as unto the Lord"? This, in the same book, Ephesians, which tells children to obey their parents and tells servants to be obedient to their masters. Somehow, women, along with children and servants, end up subjects in the master-subject relationship.

The idea that women are to play a subservient role and not to be taken seriously has been perpetuated through the use of the word "lady." One might, at first glance, think that referring to a woman as a "lady" is something complimentary and desirable. Upon closer examination, however, "lady" turns out to be a verbal label connoting the non-seriousness of women.

Robin Lakoff has argued convincingly that "lady" is a euphemism. Of the euphemism generally she declares:

"When a word acquires a bad connotation by association with something people find unpleasant or embarrassing to think of, people will reach for substitutes for that word that do not have this uncomfortable effect — that is, euphemisms. What then happens is that, since feelings about the things or people referred to themselves are not altered by a change of name, the new name itself takes on the same old connotations, and a new euphemisn must be found. It is no doubt possible to pick out those areas in which a society is feeling particular psychological strain or discomfort — areas where problems exist in a culture — by pinpointing those lexical items around which a great many euphemisms are clustered." [14] One has only to think of the numerous euphemisms we have for death, toilet, and certain dreaded diseases. Lakoff's point is that "unless we start feeling more respect for women, and at the same time less uncomfortable about them and their roles in society in relation to men, we cannot avoid *ladies* any more than we can avoid broads." [15]

In her discussion of the use of "lady" in job terminology,

Lakoff writes: "For at least some speakers, the more demeaning the job, the more the person holding it (if female, of course) is likely to be described as a *lady*. Thus cleaning *lady* is at least as common as *cleaning woman*, *saleslady* as *saleswoman*. But one says, normally *woman doctor*. To say *lady doctor* is to be very condescending; it constitutes an insult. For men, there is no such dichotomy. *Garbage man* or *salesman* is the only possibility, never *garbage gentleman*." [16]

The non-seriousness of "lady" as contrasted to "woman" is exemplified further in the titles of organizations: "It seems that organizations of women who have a serious purpose (not merely that of spending time with one another) cannot use the word *lady* in their titles, but less serious ones may. Compare the *Ladies' Auxiliary* of a men's group, or the *Thursday Evening Ladies Browning and Garden Society* with *Ladies' Lib* or *Ladies Strike for Peace*." [17]

One might try substituting "ladies" for "women" in the following: National Organization for Women; Harvard Medical and Dental School Committee on the Status of Women; Women's Studies Program; Radical Women; Black Women's Community Development Foundation. One seldom finds "lady" or "ladies" in titles of books which treat women seriously; substituting those terms for "woman" or "women" in the following titles clearly demonstrates that "lady" trivializes, denegrates: *The Natural Superiority of Women* by M. F. Ashley Montague; *Women and the Law* by Leo Kanowitz; *A Vindication of the Rights of Women* by Mary Wollstonecraft; *The Subjection of Women* by John S. Mill; *The Emancipation of Women* by V. I. Lenin; *The Ideas of the Woman Suffrage Movement* by Aileen Kraditor.

To those who say that the use of "lady" is simply a matter of being polite, Lakoff answers: "The concept of politeness thus invoked is the politeness used in dignifying or ennobling a concept that normally is not thought of as having dignity or nobility. It is this notion of politeness that explains why we have *cleaning lady*, but not normally *lady doctor*: a doctor does not need to be exalted by conventional expressions: she has dignity enough from her professional status. But a cleaning woman is in a very different situation, in which her occupational category requires ennobling. Then perhaps we can say that the very notion of womanhood, as opposed to manhood, requires ennobling since it lacks inherent dignity of its own; hence the word *woman* requires the existence of a euphemism like *lady*." [18]

The euphemistic word does more than communicate information; it defines and shapes our ideas about women and our behavior towards them. Ralph Woods has stated that "in the midst of the dangers, alarms and complexities of modern life it is easy to overlook this penchant for euphemisms — pastel words used to gloss over an ugly, unpleasant or unpopular fact, practice, or situation, and with the softer term obscure or understate the truth." [19] What we have done with the "softer term" *lady* is to obscure and understate the importance of women, their status, their contributions. While the euphemism "lady" has been used to "dignify" the woman, it has also been used to undercut her seriousness and significance.

The practice of placing the words "lady," "woman," or "female" before "doctors," "dean," "editor," "reporter," et cetera leads to (1) acceptance of the idea that unless the identifying female term is present, the professional is a man, and (2) emphasizing the sexual over the professional. Lakoff cites the example of atheist Madalyn Murray O'Hair being identified in the *San Francisco Chronicle* as the "lady atheist" and then points out that "even *woman atheist* is scarcely defensible: first, because her sex is irrelevant to her philosophical position, and second, because her name makes it clear in any event." [20]

Jessica Murray in her article "Male Perspective in Language" reprints a poem by Elsa King illustrating this questionable practice of prefixing occupational terms with "lady," "woman," and "female":

> *When I grow up I want to be a female vocalist.*
> *When I grow up I want to be a lady veterinarian.*
> *When I grow up I want to be a woman lawyer.*
> *When I grow up I want to be a boy doctor.*
> *. . . and they'll say that's redundant.*[21]

The labels "woman dean" or "lady doctor" magnify the sex of the professional at the expense of the more important attributes of the person involved. Labels of primary potency, writes Gordon Allport, "act like shrieking sirens, deafening us to all the finer discriminations that we might otherwise perceive." [22] When *Time* magazine reported that "Bobby Rogers, 31, Negro superintendent of a grubby South Bronx tenement, sprayed the street with bullets from a sawed-off .30 cal. semiautomatic carbine, killing three men and wounding a fourth," the word "Negro" stood out as a label of primary potency. (See chapter on language of white racism.) Similarly, the label of primary potency is operating when a *New York Times Magazine* article reports that "a veteran lady reporter had a longer perspective of déjà vu. 'I can remember in 1948 Muriel handing out recipes for Hubert Humphrey's Home-on-the Range Stew.'" [23]

Linguistically, we live in a world of professional men and only men; unless the professional is identified as a "lady" or "woman" we assume the person to be a male. As Casey Miller and Kate Swift have observed: "When a woman or girl makes news, her sex is identified at the beginning of a story, if possible in the headline or its equivalent. The

assumption, apparently, is that whatever event or action is
being reported, a woman's involvement is less common and
therefore more newsworthy than a man's. If the story is
about achievement, the media have developed a special and
extensive vocabulary to avoid the constant repetition of
'woman.' The results, 'Grandmother Wins Nobel Prize,'
'Blonde Hijacks Airliner,' 'Housewife to Run for Congress,'
convey the kind of information that would be ludicrous in
comparable headlines if the subjects were men." [24]

The nonseriousness and the triviality of women and their
accomplishments have been further conveyed in that special
language used to describe females in news features which
report on their personal and sexual characteristics, a language
seldom ever used in news features about men.

More often than not, the woman is identified in terms of
her husband, while the story about a man usually makes no
reference to his wife. For example, "in the recent discussion
of possible Supreme Court nominees, one woman was mentioned prominently. In discussing her general qualifications
for the office, and her background, *The New York Times*
saw fit to remark on her 'bathing-beauty figure.' Note that
is not only a judgment on a physical attribute totally removed from her qualifications for the Supreme Court, but
that it is couched in terms of how a man would react to her
figure, rather than being merely descriptive. So it is con-
ceivable that a male prospective nominee might (but was
not) have been described by the *Times* as 'well-preserved,'
or 'athletic,' the reference in this case not invoking a judgment
on the part of the opposite sex, and not as 'sexy'; but a
woman appointee is described as though an entrant in a
beauty contest: even an aspirant to a Supreme Court seat
is judged in terms of her physical attractiveness to men." [25]

Commenting on this double standard treatment, one time

Presidential press secretary Bill Moyers has said: "The obsolete treatment of women in the press has, I think contributed greatly to the anger many women feel. Why does the press identify Golda Meir as a grandmother but not Georges Pompidou as a grandfather? Why does the press talk of a female politician's hair coloring and dress style, but not the hair dye or tailor used by a Presidential candidate or Senator?" [26]

News and feature stories about women tell us about their facial characteristics, their apartments, their clothes, their hairstyles — all trivialities which one would be surprised to find in a news story about a man. The following appeared in the *New York Times:* "At 34, Patricia Ellsberg is one of those retiring, whispery-voiced women who are usually described as 'extremely feminine.' Her face appeared untouched by make-up, and her shoulder-length hair was worn in a casual, wash-in-the-shower-and-let-it dry style. Her turquoise cotton dress was simple and plainly styled; so was her gold wedding band." As if to compound the feminity, the *New York Times* tells us that "Patricia Ellsberg pooh-poohed the stories that she was the major reason her husband switched from being a hawk to a dove on the Vietnam war." [27] It is unlikely that an article about Daniel Ellsberg would tell us about his coiffure or that he "pooh-poohed" anything.

The language of sexism not only portrays women as nonserious, as trivial, and as the "second sex," but it also contributes to her invisibility. In a world of "chairmen," "spokesmen," "statesmen," "repairmen," et cetera, the woman loses visibility. We know of the Neanderthal Man, the Java Man, and the Cro-Magnon Man, but never have we had a comparable pre-historic woman. The invisible woman remains linguistically invisible as long as "the assumption is that unless otherwise identified, people in general — including doctors and beggars — are men. It is a semantic mechanism that operates to keep women invisible: *man* and *mankind* represent everyone; *he* in generalized use refers to either sex; the 'land where our fathers died' is also the land of our mothers — although they go unsung." [28]

This invisibility of women was clearly demonstrated in a one page anti-war ad which appeared in the *New York Times* on April 4, 1971. The ad was composed of a half-page drawing of President Nixon with huge corks in his ears. Over the drawing were the words: "THE MAJORITY IS NOT SILENT. THE ADMINISTRATION IS DEAF." About a dozen men are shown attempting to get the corks out of Nixon's ears. Nowhere in this anti-war ad is it suggested that women have been part of the majority which is "not silent" — part of that group trying to uncork Nixon's ears. Considering the important roles played by women in the anti-Vietnam war movement, this is indeed odd.

In the world of national politics, "the battle for men's minds" suggests that women have no minds. Even in the everyday world of memos the women remain invisible:

"*To:* Deans, Directors, Chairmen, and Advisers

"*Re:* Minority Student Awards

"*Gentlemen:* Letters of nomination are now being. . . ."

One aspect of our linguistic behavior which has had considerable effect on the manner in which women have been and are perceived is the language of the law. The language of sexism has been institutionalized in the law, the statutes and court opinions defining, portraying, and stereotyping women as mindless, weak, immoral, pure, and incompetent, like children, idiots, and drunkards.

Like children — unable physically and mentally to cope with some of the more serious aspects of life, unable to protect themselves, weak and susceptible — women have been defined by the language of the law as inferior to men. One of the many anachronisms of the law is the legal placement of the woman on a pedestal by prohibiting her to foul herself with "man's work" and by protecting her from the obscene language of the "man's world." Through the language of the law sexism has been institutionalized by legally portraying the woman as on the one hand the powerful evil temptress and on the other hand as the pure, weak untarnished mother up on a pedestal.

But the pedestal, upon closer examination, is a kind of prison as the California Supreme Court pointed out in declaring unconstitutional a state law which prohibited the employment of women as bartenders "Laws which disable women from full participation in the political, business and economic arenas are often characterized as 'protective' and beneficial. Those same laws applied to racial or ethnic minorities would readily be recognized as invidious and impermissible. The pedestal upon which women have been placed has all too often upon closer inspection been revealed as a cage." [29] This realization did not come about until 1971.

Past court opinions and state statutes abound in which women and children and sometimes the insane are all thrown in together. In 1964 the United States Court of Appeals, Fifth Circuit, in deciding that a married woman in Texas could not be held to a contract because of her sex-marital status, said: "This is a simple case of trying to hold a married woman liable on a contract which under the laws of Texas she was incapable of making, and the claim is no more reasonable than to hold a minor, or one of unsound mind, could be held liable on a contract despite his disability merely because the United States was a party to it." [30]

Two years later the United States Supreme Court upheld

the Court of Appeals decision, but Justices William O. Douglas and Byron White joined Justice Hugo Black in a dissent in which Black wrote: "The Texas law of 'coverture,' which was adopted by its judges and which the State's legislature has now largely abandoned, rests on the old common-law fiction that the husband and wife are one. This rule has worked out in reality to mean that though the husband and wife are one, the one is the husband. This fiction rested on what I had supposed is today a completely discredited notion that a married woman, being a female, is without capacity to make her own contracts and do her own business. . . . It seems at least unique to me that this court in 1966 should exalt this archaic remnant of a primitive caste system to an honored place among the laws of the United States." [81]

If the woman was defined in Texas as being "without capacity to make her own contracts," like minors and people of unsound mind, she was defined in the state of Washington, until 1969, as a person who could not be served liquor in a hotel or restaurant "except when seated at tables." When the Washington Supreme Court held legal the requirement "that intoxicating liquor may be dispensed to women only when they are seated," it concluded that the requirement violates no constitutional right of either the licensee or the women and is a regulation that was within the power of the state to make." [82]

To support its position, the Washington Supreme Court cited earlier decisions, one being a 1902 Colorado decision dealing with the conviction of a Denver saloon keeper who had admitted women into his "wine room"; the language of the Colorado Supreme Court is revealing: "If a discrimination is made against women solely on account of their sex, it would not be good; but if it is because of the immorality that would be likely to result if the regulation was not made, the regulation would be sustained. That injury to public morality would ensue if women were permitted without restrictions to frequent wine rooms, there to be supplied with liquor, is so apparent to the average person that argument to establish so plain a proposition is unnecessary." [33]

After pointing out this "self evident truth," the Colorado court then went on to say that many states have regulations which legislatures have passed in the interests of good morals, the court comparing the rights of women with those of slaves, minors, Indians, and habitual drunkards: "The laws of many states prohibit the sale of intoxicating liquors to Indians, minors, habitual drunkards, and other classes of people, and in many of the Southern states before the Civil War sales to slaves and free Negroes were forbidden." [34] Once this kind of classification of women was legally accepted, it was but a small step to denying them equal rights with men, white men.

A considerable number of turn-of-the-century court opinions, like the Colorado opinion, placed the women in the same class as infants and the immoral, with the effect of prohibiting women from certain jobs and actions. In 1902 the New Jersey Supreme Court in deciding to uphold an ordinance which prohibited women (except wives of tavern owners) to be bartenders, linked women with immorality; it seems to me, said the judge delivering the opinion of the court, "that there is just ground for the discrimination of this ordinance. The supposed evil aimed at is the employment of women in connection with a traffic likely to induce vice and immorality. The wife of a proprietor of a place of public entertainment is not, in any fair sense, an employee, and her presence may fairly be deemed to be deterrent to impropriety." [35]

In 1906 the Court of Appeals of Kentucky upheld an
ordinance which read: "It shall be unlawful for any infant
or female to go into or be in or drink intoxicating liquors in
any saloon or place for sale of such liquors, or any room
used in connection with and opening into such saloon or
place for the sale of such liquors, or in any billiard or
poolroom within the city" of Madisonville, Kentucky. In
declaring the ordinance legally valid, the Kentucky court,
like the Colorado court, accepted the "well-known fact that
the frequenting of saloons by lewd women tends to immorality." [36]

The Kentucky court portrayed women as being in the same
class as infants and also as carriers of immorality: "The
ordinance in question only prohibits the saloon keeper from
suffering or permitting infants or women to drink in the
saloon or to be or remain therein over five minutes, and it
provides that it shall be a defense if the person charged should
show that the infant or female was in good repute, and was at
the time sober and orderly, and had the consent of the parent
or guardian of the infant or husband of the female, or in
case of reasonable necessity. It is a well-known fact that the
frequenting of saloons by lewd women tends to immorality,
and that the frequenting of saloons by infants is not pro-
motive of good citizenship." [37]

For too long the courts have placed the onus of immorality
on the female; it is the woman's presence at the tavern which
leads to the licentiousness, and the resulting argument is
that by prohibiting the woman from the tavern we are keeping away sin. Why is it that the frequenting of saloons by
lewd women tends to immorality, but the frequenting of
saloons by lewd men does not? While the woman has been
defined by law as the delicate creature needing protection,

she has also been defined as the wicked creature who can bring injury to public morality.

In some respects things improved by 1970. A federal court, in deciding that a state could not sanction sexual segregation in public facilities such as alehouses, said in 1970: "Nor do we find any merit in the argument that the presence of women in bars gives rise to 'moral and social problems' against which McSorley's can reasonably protect itself by excluding women from the premises.... Outdated images of bars as dens of coarseness and iniquity and of women as peculiarly delicate and impressionable creatures in need of protection from the rough and tumble of unvarnished humanity will no longer justify sexual separatism." [38]

In 1971 the California Supreme Court rejected that state's argument that it had an interest in prohibiting women from bartending; the two interests served were, according to the state, "first women who do not have an interest by way of ownership or marriage in the liquor license will not be sufficiently restrained from committing 'improprieties,' and second, that women bartenders would be an 'unwholesome influence' on young people and the general public." [39]

The first rationale, said the California court, "rests upon the peculiar and wholly unacceptable generalization that women in bars, unrestrained by husbands or the risk of losing a liquor license, will commit improper acts. This rationale fails as a compelling state interest because it is wholly arbitrary and without support in logic or experience." "The second rationale — that women bartenders would be an 'unwholesome influence' on the public —is even weaker than the first," said the court, arguing that the objection to women tending bars "appears to be based upon notions of what is a 'ladylike' or proper pursuit for a woman in our society rather than any accertainable evil effects of permitting women to labor behind those 'permanently affixed fixtures' known as bars." [40]

Besides having been definitionally thrown in with children, the insane, habitual drunkards, and slaves in relation to contractural rights and liquor restrictions, women have been and still are identified with children in matters dealing with obscenity. When it comes to obscenity, First Amendment rights do not apply equally to women and men. State statutes which prohibit the expression of obscenities in the presence of women and children do not prohibit that same expression when only men are present. Leo Kanowitz has stated that "the juxtaposition of women and children as the persons to be spared the ordeal of hearing obscene, vulgar or abusive words is reminiscent of the common law's time-honored practice of treating women like infants or, at times, idiots." [41]

The Penal Code of California specifies that every person who uses "any vulgar, profane, or indecent language within the presence or hearing of women or children" is guilty of a misdemeanor. Arizona's Revised Statutes (1956), Section 13-377 also attempts to protect women and children from obscene language: "A person who, in the presence or hearing of any woman or child, or in a public place, uses vulgar, abusive or obscene language, is guilty of a misdemeanor."

Kanowitz has pointed out that "the only explanation for such interests is that once more they express social attitudes that women are essentially of a different species than men, that they are brittle objects to be spared the reality of everyday living, and they are in a fundamental sense second-class citizens — all of which raise serious questions concerning the ability of such laws to withstand attacks on due process and equal protection grounds." [42] Some of our obscenity laws say, in effect, that like children, but unlike adult men, adult women are incapable of handling the rough and tumble

THE LANGUAGE OF SEXISM

language of everyday life. The irony is that the woman who has been defined by the language of the law as the carrier of immorality and wickedness has also been defined as one to be protected from wicked and immoral language.

Women and children are classed together not only in obscenity statutes, but also in court opinions dealing with obscenity. In April, 1968, Paul Cohen wore a jacket bearing the words "Fuck the Draft" while walking down the corridor of the Los Angeles Courthouse. In denying First Amendment protection to Cohen's message of protest, the California Appellate Court declared: "The gravamen for the defendant's offense was his selection of the public corridors of the county courthouse as the place to parade before women and children who were involuntarily subjected to unprintable language." [43] The Court said that "no one has the right to express his views by means of printing lewd and vulgar language which is likely to cause others to breach of the peace to protect women and children from such exposure." [44]

When the case reached the United States Supreme Court, the majority found for Cohen and against the State of California, Justice John Harlan speaking for the majority stating the "surely the State has no right to cleanse public debate to the point where it is grammatically palatable to the most squeamish among us" and that "while the particular four-letter word being litigated here is perhaps more distasteful than most others of its genre, it is nevertheless often true that one man's vulgarity is another's lyric." [45]

Women and children, in the eyes of Chief Justice Warren Burger, played an important role in a case dealing with a speech delivered at "a public school board meeting attended by about 150 people, approximately 40 of whom were children and 25 of whom were women. In the course of his remarks he [speaker Rosenfeld] used the adjective 'M —

F —' on four occasions, to describe the teachers, the school board, the town and his own country." [46]

Referring to the Rosenfeld case, the Chief Justice said: "... civilized people attending such a meeting with wives and children would not likely have an instantaneous, violent response, but it does not unduly tax the imagination to think that some justifiably outraged parent whose family were exposed to the foul mouthings of the speaker would 'meet him outside' and either alone or with others, resort to the 19th century's vigorous modes of dealing with such people." [47] To protect women and children from hearing "foul mouthings" the Chief Justice would deny First Amendment protection to a speaker who would apparently get constitutional protection if his audience were composed only of men.

One of the effects of defining women as persons to be protected from the realities and vulgarities of a "man's world" was to deny suffrage and jury participation to women. As late as 1966, Justice Jones of the Mississippi Supreme Court wrote in his opinion upholding that state's statute excluding women from jury duty: "The legislature has the right to exclude women so they may continue their service as mothers, wives, and homemakers, and also to protect them (in some areas, they are still upon a pedestal) from the filth, obscenity, and noxious atmosphere that so often pervades a courtroom during a jury trial." [48]

Anti-suffragists had argued for decades that woman's place was in the home, supplementing this argument with one which concluded that women's suffrage would lead adult females into indecencies and vulgarities that were not compatable with their place high on the pedestal. In editorializing against the 19th century feminists, the *New York Herald* said in September 1852: "What do the leaders of the Woman's

Rights Convention want? They want to vote, and to hustle with the rowdies at the polls. They want to be members of Congress, and in the heat of debate to subject themselves to coarse jeers and indecent language." [49]

Arguing against granting the vote to women, Representative Clark of Florida said in 1915: "I do not wish to see the day come when the women of my race in my state shall trail their skirts in the muck and mire of partisan politics. I prefer to look to the American woman as she always has been, occupying her proud estate as the queen of the American home, instead of regarding her as a ward politician in the cities. As the mother, wife, as the sister she exercises a broader and deeper and mightier influence than she can ever exercise or hope to on the stump and in the byways of politics in this land. The American mother, the American woman, has my admiration, my respect, and my love. . . . " [50]

Having placed the woman on a pedestal, the man proceeds to protect her from filthy, indecent, and vulgar language, whether in the halls of Congress, in the jury room, or in the public at large. "The natural and proper timidity and delicacy which belongs to the female sex evidently unfits it for many of the occupations of civil life," [51] said the United States Supreme Court in 1872, deciding that women could be legally prohibited from practicing law in Illinois. One of the Justices asserted in his concurring opinion: "The paramount destiny and mission of women are to fulfill the noble and benign offices of wife and mother. This is the law of the creator. And the rules of civil society must be adapted to the general constitution of things. . . . " [52]

Almost a century later the United States Supreme Court was still defining the proper place of women as being in the home. In a 1961 decision dealing with a woman who had killed her husband with a baseball bat and was subsequently tried by an all male jury, the Supreme Court said:

"Despite the enlightened emancipation of women from the restrictions and protections of bygone years, and their entry into many parts of community life formerly considered to be reserved for men, woman is still regarded as the center of home and family life. We cannot say that it is constitutionally impermissible for a State, acting in pursuit of the general welfare, to conclude that a woman should be relieved from the civic duty of jury service unless she herself determines that such service is consistent with her own special responsibilities." [53]

(Florida's all male jury resulted from a Florida statute stipulating "that the name of no female shall be taken for jury service unless said person has registered with the clerk of the circuit court her desire to be placed on the jury list"; while only registered females can serve on the jury all males of the state are automatically eligible for jury duty).

The Supreme Court rejected the appellant's argument that "the nature of the crime of which she was convicted peculiarly demanded the inclusion of persons of her own sex on the jury." The killing had taken place in "the context of a marital upheavel involving, among other things, the suspected infidelity of appellant's husband, and culminating in the husband's final rejection of his wife's efforts at reconciliation." [54] The Court found Florida's law requiring women interested in jury duty to register, while men automatically were placed on the jury list, constitutional, even though a consequence of this selection system is predominately male juries. The appellant's claim "that women jurors would have been more understanding or compassionate than men" in assessing her "crime" was rejected by the Court.

The courts and legislatures having defined woman's place as in the home, away from the "vulgarities" of life, seemingly have placed her on a pedestal but the height of that pedestal is illusory. The woman has been placed on the same pedestal level with the child. The males will be the protectors of woman and child alike. The males will see to it that women and children will not be exposed to coarseness, indecent and obscene language. The males will recognize the weakness and vulnerability of women and children.

At first glance it appears inconsistent that men would place on a pedestal something inferior to themselves or even more wicked than themselves. But on close examination the pedestal becomes recognizable as a male creation, a male definition. The woman is high enough on the pedestal to be protected from indecent and obscene language ("Fuck you!" or "Motherfucker" or "Shit on you!"), yet she is defined as the person who is expected, even required, to change the "shit-filled" diapers, and is traditionally expected, required, to submit to the "fucking" of her husband, whether he be in a drunken or "vulgar" condition. The pedestal does little to protect the woman from the actual "filth and vulgarities" of life. In the name of protecting the woman from the *language* of filth, obscenity, and immorality, from the *language* which "so often pervades the courtroom during a jury trial," from the indecent *language* heard in the halls of Congress, the men have denied women full participation in serious decision-making processes. The pedestal, in effect, has been a tool for suppression.

Shulamith Firestone has commented on the pedestal status of women and children in her book *The Dialectic of Sex.* In discussing similarities between the treatment of children and the working class she writes: "One didn't discuss serious matters nor did one curse in front of women and children. . . . (As for the double standard about cursing: A man is allowed to blaspheme the world because it belongs to him to damn —

but the same curse out of the mouth of a woman or a minor, i.e., an incomplete 'man' to whom the world does not yet belong, is considered presumptuous, and thus an impropriety or worse.) Both were set apart by fancy and nonfunctional clothing and were given special tasks (housework and homework respectively); both were considered mentally deficient ('What can you expect from a woman?' 'He's too little to understand.'). The pedestal of adoration on which both were set aside made it hard for them to breath. . . ." [55]

The serious establishment of a woman's self-identity has been hampered not only by the language of the law which has trivialized the status of women, but her search for identity has been interfered with by the ritual of women adopting the names of their husbands upon marriage. William Blackstone, eighteenth century English jurist and legal scholar, wrote in his influential *Commentaries:* "By marriage the husband and wife are one person in law; that is the very being or legal existence of the woman is suspended during the marriage, or at least is incorporated and consolidated into that of the husband; under whose wing, protection, and cover, she performs everything; and is therefore called in our law — French, a feme-covert. . . . said to be a covert-baron, or under the protection and influence of her husband, her baron, or lord. . . ."

Part of the suspension of the woman's "very being or legal existence" is the relinquishing of her "maiden name" for the name of her husband. This ritual has its male supremist implications, like the ritual of giving the newborn child the male parent's surname.

"What's In A Name?" asks Julie Coryell in the winter 1971 issue of *Women: A Journal of Liberation.* Her answer: "Plenty. Why is it that women take their husband's name on marriage? Why do we call our original names maiden names? Why don't we keep our names if we want to? In studying about patriarchy, I learned that women and children came to bear the husband's name and father's name be-because he owned them. I am no one's possession but my own self. Social usage clarifies the potential sexual availability of a woman in her name. We are Miss so and so — fair game — or Mrs. (man's name) — safe, hands off, men — or Mrs. (woman's name) — divorced? Available? Probably. Mr. does not reveal a man's marital status. After all, what does marital status have to do with one's work and attitudes? Why must women continue to be forced to declare it unless it is truly relevant?" [56]

The institution of marriage has allowed the male to remain a "man" but the female must undergo change from "woman" to "wife" and traditionally undergoes a change from her "maiden" name to her husband's name. The minister says, "Do you take this woman to be your wife?" and then turns to the woman and asks "Do you take this man to be your husband?" After both have said "I do" they are informed that they are now "man and wife."

Some progress was made in May 1972 when it was announced that "Lutheran fathers are no longer able to give their daughters away in marriage." [75] The Director of the Commission on Worship of the Lutheran Church in America explained: "The bride is not the property of her father to be turned over to the husband whose property she becomes." [58] The wife, whatever marriage ritual is followed, then adopts her "man's" last name, exchanging one male's surname for another male's surname. While the law generally allows a person to change one's name or to retain one's "maiden" name, there are some areas in the law where the woman must use her husband's name.

In September 1972 the Attorney General of Connecticut

ruled that a married woman must use her husband's last name when she registers to vote.[59] In September 1971 a three judge Federal Court ruled in Montgomery, Alabama that a married woman does not have a constitutional right to a driver's license issued in her maiden name.[60]

Although Gunnar Mydral discusses in his classic work *An American Dilemma* the similarities in the treatment of blacks and women in the United States, he fails to mention that a similarity between these two groups is that they both have been given the names of their "masters." The black slave's identity was related directly to the owner of the slave; the identity of the woman is established by virtue of her relationship to men, and not vice versa.

Lakoff has pointed out that "if a man does not marry, he still has his own identity; he is not hurt by his status. But if a woman is not married, she is in many important ways an unperson. It is not usual to define a woman's position in terms of her own accomplishments, and there is no one else whose accomplishments she can gain identity from if she is not connected somehow to a man, the more firmly the better." [61]

Several writers have commented on the importance of the ritual of the married woman taking her husband's name and the impact of the name change on the woman. Kanowitz asserts that "the probable effects of this unilateral name change upon the relations between the sexes, though subtle in character, are profound. In a very real sense the loss of a woman's surname represents the destruction of an important part of her personality and its submersion in that of her husband." [62]

There is little doubt that an individual's name change has an effect on self-identity; Joyce Hertzler has observed that "an especially intriguing sociological aspect of names is the relationship of the change of name and the change of identity, of ego, and of the social status of the person. A name carries with it certain evaluations made by the named one himself, as well as the evaluations of others regarding him. A change of name invariably means some change in these evaluations. . . . When a woman takes her husband's name upon marrying him, she undergoes certain transformations of ego, as well as leaving the circle of her original family and assuming the status of a married woman, as her new name shows." [63]

As far as the law is concerned it is the male, father and husband, who has had the last word on what names the women and children shall bear. Kanowitz cites several laws and court decisions of the past which have reflected this power of defining through naming. On the basis of his examination of the law, he concludes that "under many of the statutes that prescribe formal procedures for changing one's name, the right to do so has been expressly or impliedly denied to married women. No comparable restriction has been imposed upon married men. Finally, the law, once more either expressly or by implication, generally requires that a change in the husband's surname produce a corresponding change in that of his wife, but never the reverse." [64]

Not only does the woman become lost in the anonymity of her husband's name, but as Faith Seidenberg has stated, "her domicile is his no matter where she lives, which means she cannot vote or run for office in her place of residence if her husband lives elsewhere. If she wants an annulment and is over eighteen, in certain cases she cannot get one, but her husband can until he is twenty-one. In practice, if not in theory, she cannot contract for any large amount, borrow money, or get a credit card in her own name. She is, in fact, a non-person with no name." [65] What has occurred over the decades and centuries is that linguistically the law has institutionalized the language of sexism, and when the law gave the male the power to name the female it served to perpetuate his status of master in the master-subject relationship.

The woman's efforts to achieve self-identity has been further complicated by the "street language" which labels her a sexual child object. She is openly called "babe," "toots," "chick," "doll," et cetera. All of these labels are associated with children, helplessness, and immaturity.

Dictionary definitions tell us a "babe" is "1. a baby; infant; hence, 2. a naive, gullible, or helpless person. 3. [slang], a girl or young woman, especially a pretty one." A "chick" is "1. a young chicken. 2. a young bird. 3. a child: term of endearment." A "tootsy" is "1. a child's or woman's small foot. 2. "toots"; and a "toots" is "[slang], darling, dear: affectionate or playful term of address." If a woman is not a "babe," "toots," or "chick," she can be a "doll." Doll: "1. a children's toy made to resemble a baby, child or grown person. 2. a pretty but rather stupid or silly girl or woman. 3. a pretty child. 4. [slang], any girl or young woman." And if the woman is not labeled any of these, she still can be a "girl." No matter how high in professional status or how old she may be, the woman can always be the "girl."

Three of the definitions of "girl" given by *Webster's New World Dictionary of the American Language* are: "1. a female child. 2. a young, unmarried woman. 3. a female servant." Lakoff has said of the use of the term "girl": "One seldom hears a man past the age of adolescence referred to as a boy, save in expressions like 'going out with boys,' which are meant to suggest an air of adolescent frivolity and irresponsibility. But women of all ages are 'girls'.... It may be that this use of *girl* is euphemistic in the sense in which *lady* is an euphemism: in stressing the idea of immaturity, it removes the sexual connotations lurking in women." [66]

All of these terms identifying women with babies and children result in a portrayal of mature females as weak, silly, irresponsible and dependent. The women are infantalized through language.

The language of sexism, like the language of racism, leads to circularity in our thinking and behavior. Our sexist language does affect our attitudes and behavior which in turn affect our language. What Diana Schulder has said about sexual discrimination and the law applies equally to discrimination and language: "prejudice (the mythology of class oppression) is enshrined in laws. Laws lead to enforcement or practices. Practices reinforce and lead to prejudice. The cycle continues...." [67]

Frantz Fanon has insightfully discussed the effects of such circularity in perpetuating racism. What he has to say is relevant to the language of sexism and warrants repeating. Racist language, he declares, has the effect of "classifying," "imprisoning," "primitivizing," and "decivilizing" the blacks. If a doctor greets a black patient with "You not feel good, no?" or "G'morning pal. Where's it hurt? Huh? Lemme see — belly ache? Heart pain?" the doctor feels perfectly justified in speaking that way, writes Fanon, when in return the patient answers in the same fashion; the doctor can then say to himself, "You see I wasn't kidding you. That's the way they are."

To make the black person talk pidgin, as Fanon observes, "is to fasten him to the effigy of him, to snare him, to imprison him, the eternal victim of an essence, of an *appearance* for which he is not responsible." (See chapter on the language of white racism.) Whites have in effect encouraged and perpetuated outdated stereotypes of blacks through the manner in which they speak about and to blacks. If Fanon is correct, the whites by 'talking down" to the blacks are telling them to "remember where you come from!" Similarly, through the language of sexism, males by "talking down" to the females are telling them to "remember your place!"

If one may be allowed a little optimism, notwithstanding all that has been said above, it may be a new day. The shift away from the courts' defining woman as immature, as incapable of dealing with the serious aspects of life, as standing on a pedestal confined to the status of homemaker, as the carrier of wickedness and immorality, the shift away from defining woman as inferior to man and towards the woman as a self-defined human being may be upon us and here to stay. In 1973 a majority of the U. S. Supreme Court admitted for the first time in its history that perhaps the place of the woman was not confined to the home and that there is a viciousness in treating all women as an inferior class which does not take into account the individual. "Statutory distinctions between the sexes," said the Court majority, "often have the effect of invidiously relegating the entire class of females to inferior legal status without regard to the actual capabilities of its individual members." [68]

6

THE LANGUAGE OF WAR

Resources control. . .regrettable by-products. . .impact area
. . .hardware. . .hornets' nests. . .protective reaction. . .pacifi-
cation. . .strategic hamlet. . .New Life Hamlet. . .incursion. . .
Operation Ranch Hand. . .Operation Independence. . .Opera-
tion Sunrise. . .defoliation. . .advisers.

If one did not know better one would never suspect a war
was going on, that human beings were being mutilated,
tortured, forcibly removed from their villages, wounded, and
killed. This was the language of a war in which 60,000
United States soldiers and "advisers" were killed, in which
over one million Vietnamese soldiers were killed. The words
and terms used by governmental officials to report what was
occurring in Vietnam and Southeast Asia between 1962 and
1972 constitute an excellent case study in how language is
corrupted to mask the cruelty and inhumanity of war, to
attempt to justify the unjustifiable.

Linguistically legitimatizing the killing of "the enemy"
during wartime has long been a preoccupation of military
and civilian officials bent on waging war. Language is the
tool to be used to make acceptable what civilized people would
ordinarily not see as acceptable.

"War," according to Aldous Huxley, "is enormously dis-
creditable to those who order it to be waged and even to
those who merely tolerate its existence. Furthermore, to developed sensibilities the facts of war are revolting and horri-
fying. . . . By suppressing and distorting the truth, we protect our sensibilities and preserve our self-esteem. Now,
language is, among other things, a device men use for

suppressing and distorting the truth. Finding the reality of war too unpleasant to contemplate, we create a verbal alternative to that reality, parallel with it, but in quality quite different from it. That which we contemplate thenceforth is not that to which we react emotionally and upon which we pass our moral judgments, is not war as it is in fact, but the fiction of war as it exists in our pleasantly falsifying verbiage." [1]

In his now famous essay "Politics and the English Language," George Orwell pointed out that "political speech and writing are largely the defense of the indefensible.... Defenseless villages are bombarded from the air, the inhabitants driven out into the country-side, the cattle machine-gunned, the huts set on fire with incendiary bullets: this is called *pacification*." [2]

Huxley's and Orwell's observations were especially relevant during the decade of United States military involvement in Southeast Asia. In 1972 Representative Robert F. Drinan of Massachusetts told an audience of English professors: "It is my duty to report to you that the objects of Orwell's observation are at this moment comfortably ensconced in the State and Defense Departments and, ironically or predictably, they are the very individuals who in so many other respects are bringing us closer to the Orwellian version of a sterile 1984." [3] Regarding the deceptive use of language in describing the Vietnam War Peter Farb observed: "The predominant strategy was the ornate euphemism — an effort to divert attention from the true horrors of death and destruction by labeling something the opposite of what it truly was. An aggressive attack by an armada of airplanes, which most speakers of English call simply an *air raid*, was instead spoken of as a momentary defensive strategy, a *routine limited duration protective reaction*. Defoliation of an entire forest, with the result that it may not sprout another green leaf for decades or even hundreds of years, was labeled a *resources control program.*" [4]

During the war in Indochina the American military took words which carried connotations of peace, nonviolence, and conciliation and used them to hide cruelty and inhumanity inflicted on the Vietnamese people. A "pacification" program was established and month after month, year after year, government officials declared, as in some primitive incantation, that the United States was making "progress in pacification."

Writing of the situation in 1962, David Halberstam reported in his *The Making of a Quagmire:* "Some general or official would arrive in Vietnam, would spend one day in Saigon being briefed and meeting the Ngo family, and another day or two in the field inspecting selected strategic-hamlets and units. Then he would hold an airport press conference in which he would say that the war was being won, that the people were rallying to the government, that he had been impressed by the determination of President Diem, who was a great leader." All through 1963 officials in Saigon and Washington, D. C. recited the words, "We are winning in Vietnam." When in May, 1964, South Vietnamese General Khanh took the offensive and South Vietnamese casualties began to rise, the Pentagon reported that the General was "on the right track." In August, 1965, officials in Saigon and Washington expressed exuberant optimism over the course of the war. And in July 1966, Vice-President Hubert Humphrey declared: "We are gaining on all four major fronts — the economic front, the political front, the diplomatic front and the military front."

Late in the 1960's the American people were told again and again, "We now have the initiative in Vietnam." [5] During the early 1970's high civilian and military leaders an-

nounced that the end was in sight, that "the light at the
end of the tunnel could be seen."

Official recitations and incantations about the war in
Vietnam would have done justice to any primitive medicine-
men attempting to cast a spell over members of their tribes
or over tribal enemies.

The "pacification" which officials described as progress-
ing so well turned out to be the "pacification" described by
Orwell. One journalist disclosed how this "pacifying" of
Vietnamese villages was carried out: "The Vietnamese woman
ignored the crying baby in her arms. She stared in hatred
as the American infantrymen with shotguns blasted away at
chickens and ducks. Others shot a water buffalo and a pet
dog. While her husband, father, and young son were led
away, the torch was put to the hut that contained the family
belongings. The flames consumed everything — including the
shrine to the family ancestors." [6]

"Pacification" was used as a label for actions which involved entering a village with bayonets at the ready, "per-
suading" the people to evacuate their huts, rounding up all
the males and shooting those who resisted, prodding the
elderly, the women and the children into camps set up by
the United States military, slaughtering the domesticated
animals and burning the pitiful dwellings to the ground.
A news source reported that "one village so persistently resisted pacification that finally it had to be destroyed." [7] See
Webster: Pacify: to make peaceful, calm; to tranquilize.

The forcible migration of Vietnamese civilians from their
villages to "strategic hamlets" was described in a variety of
terms to minimize the inhumanity of it all. Paul Dickson
observed in 1972 that "the forced transfer of civilians was
invariably given a nice 'operation' or 'program' title like
'Operation Independence,' or 'Operation Sunrise.' Such

transfers were officially termed 'compulsory relocation' and the civilians involved were either moved to 'strategic hamlets' or 'resettlement centers' — locales that were often no more that what they were called 'refugee camps' in other wars. As a *New York Times* reporter observed. . .'A few people were driven together, a roll of barbed wire was thrown over their heads, and the strategic hamlet was finished.' " [8]

"Pacification" in Vietnam, wrote Edward and Onora Nell in 1967, "has included at various times the construction of 'New Life Hamlets,' and of 'Prosperity Zones' containing 'strategic hamlets.' More recently a 'Rural Construction Program' came on the scene, followed by a 'Revolutionary Development Program' which in turn gave way to a 'Rural Development Program.' " [9]

What occurs when a perfectly good word like "pacification" is used as a euphemism for acts of cruelty and inhumanity is that the word loses its former meaning and cannot be uttered later without connoting some of what it attempted to hide in Vietnam. This "destruction" of words occurred in Germany under the Nazis; perfectly good words were misused and distorted with the result that after the war these same words could not be used without carrying with them the distorted meanings attributed to them by the Nazis.

Steiner has pointed out that the bestialities of Nazism infected the German language.[10] It was used "to enforce innumerable falsehoods, to persuade the Germans that the war was just and everything victorious. As defeat began closing in on the thousand-year Reich, the lies thickened to a constant snowdrift. The language was turned upside down to say 'light' where there was blackness and 'victory' where there was 'disaster.' " [11] This distorted use of language eventually has its negative effects on the language itself and as Steiner says, "there comes a breaking point. Use a language to conceive, organize, and justify Belsen; use it to make out specifications for gas ovens; use it to dehumanize man during twelve years of calculated bestiality. Something will happen to it. Make words that Hitler and Goebbels and a hundred thousand *Unterstrumführer* made: conveyors of terror and falsehood. Something will happen to the words. Something of the lies and sadism will settle in the marrow of the language." [12]

Words such as "restraint" and "protective" were debased when Richard Nixon used the former to describe United States military activities in Vietnam and when the Air Force used the latter in the term "protective reaction" to minimize large scale bombings. "Throughout the war . . .," Nixon declared on May 8, 1972, "the United States has exercised a degree of restraint unprecedented in the annals of war." But as Ronald Kriss commented in the *Saturday Review:* "Restraint? We have grown discouragingly accustomed to the abuse, misuse, and even nonuse of words. But this was a rather blatant example, even coming from a politician. I assume the President meant that because we never supported an invasion of North Vietnam, because we never breached the Red River dikes, because we never resorted to nuclear weapons, because, in short, we never totally laid waste the country, we can congratulate ourselves for our unprecedently civilized behavior." [13]

"Still," Kriss added, "it requires an extraordinary insensitivity to the language to talk of 'restraint,' when we have dumped twice as many tons of explosives on South Vietnam alone as we did in all combat zones during all of World War II, when we have contributed to the killing or maiming of hundreds of thousands — if not millions — of civilians, when we have turned countless acres of once-lush forests and farmlands into hideous moonscapes, barren and brown-hued ... Nor does the word ring true when we consider that the Vietnam War is the longest in our history and, in terms of battle deaths, the fourth-costliest (after World War II, the Civil War, and World War I, in that order.)" [14]

The extensive "protective reaction" air raids over North Vietnam were part of this "restraint." In an item titled "Terminology in Air War," the *New York Times* said on June 16, 1972: "Under 'protective reaction,' American commanders were authorized to seek out and attack enemy troops or planes or missiles that threatened them. The use of the phrase by Mr. Laird [Secretary of Defense] at the 1969 news conference marked a shift from previous American military orders in which United States ground forces were to put 'maximum pressure' on the enemy."

The *New York Times* reported that "three former members of a photo-intelligence team assigned to Pacific Air Force headquarters in Hawaii said in an interview today that at least 20 to 25 planned bombing raids later described as 'protective reaction' strikes were flown each month by Air Force planes over North Vietnam throughout 1970 and 1971 .... All three airmen interviewed today agreed that the concept of 'protective reaction' was widely considered throughout the Pacific Air Force command as simply another way of describing bombing raids." [15] One of the airmen stated: "We were constantly hitting truck depots and storage areas and describing them as P. R. strikes." Another airman, who had seen all of the pilot reports for Seventh Air Force missions flown in Laos, Cambodia and North Vietnam, said that "invariably, after such missions. ... the pilots would enter 'protective reaction' on their reports." Finally, on April 4, 1972, "the policy of 'protective reaction' was suspended with the resumption of full-scale bombing of North Vietnam after the start of the North Vietnamese offensive." [16]

The depersonalization of the Vietnamese people reached its height in the B-52 bombers which flew from Anderson Air Force Base in Guam, six hours flying time away from their targets in Vietnam, to drop their high explosive bombs on the people and land below. To the crew aboard the B-52, it had become an "impersonal war." Joseph Treaster reports that "for the crewmen, sitting in their air-conditioned compartments more than five miles above the steamy jungle of South Vietnam, the bomb run had been merely another familiar technical exercise. The crew knew virtually nothing about their target and they showed no curiosity. Only the radar-navigator, who in earlier wars would have been called the bombardier, saw the bombs exploding, and those distant flashes gave no hint of the awesome eruption of flames and steel on the ground. No one in the plane, including this correspondent, heard the deafening blast." [17] Treaster describes the effects of the exploding bombs: "On the ground a B-52 strike — or 'arclight' as they are commonly called — is a chillingly spectacular event, sometimes electric with excitement. Tremendous clouds of smoke and dust boil up and a thunder of kettle drums splits the ears. People in the 'impact' areas are killed or sent reeling in shock." [18]

None of these devastating effects were ever perceived by the men in the B-52; nothing and nobody that had been destroyed on the ground were ever seen by the airmen. One Air Force captain declared: "Essentially I feel I'm a nonparticipant in the war.... I'm intelligent and I know I'm in it, but I don't feel it." A pilot "said that he often thought of himself as a long-distance truck driver. A crewman said that bombing South Vietnam from a B-52 was like 'delivering the mail.'" Another captain stated that "if we were killing anybody down there with our bombs I have to think we were bombing the enemy and not civilians. I feel quite sure about our targetting." The killing had become so impersonal that the captain could say: "As far as losing any sleep over what we're doing, how many people we kill. . .we never get to see the damage."

Here was a war in which a B-52 pilot could say as he dropped his lethal bombs: "I am a nonparticipant in the war." [19] What higher praise is there for the success of governmental officials and technology than for a military officer to make such a statement?

Keeping the killing by ground forces impersonal has always been more difficult and therefore a variety of euphemisms have been created to conceal the reality of war. During the late 1930's, according to Aldous Huxley, militarists were "clamouring for war planes numerous and powerful enough to go and 'destroy the hornets in their nests' — in other words, to go and throw thermite, high explosives and vesicants upon the inhabitants of neighboring countries before they have time to come and do the same to us." [20]

Metaphors are used to conceal the fact that human beings are killing human beings. One military officer described the parachuting of his troops into an area occupied by the Vietcong: "Our tigers jumped from the helicopters into the VC hornets' nest." For those who like their wars less picturesque and more "sanitized" there was the suggestion that a "sanitized belt" be established stretching south of the 17th parallel at the demilitarized zone. This suggestion, made during a March 1967 meeting between Presidents Johnson and Ky meant, in effect, forcibly expelling from their homes and villages all the inhabitants of the area in question, cutting down all the trees, bulldozing the land clear, and erecting "defensive positions" provided with machine guns, mortars, and mines. See Webster: To sanitize: to bring about absence of dirt and agents of infection or disease; to promote health and healthful conditions.[21]

The bombs and other means of destruction used in the Vietnam war were given names which concealed the devastation they wreaked upon the land and the people. Sydney Schanberg reported in 1972 that American briefers in Saigon who were supposed to pass on to newsmen the "facts" about the war used a language which had "no connection with everyday English" and was "designed to sanitize the war": "Planes do not drop bombs, they 'deliver ordinance.' Napalm is a forbidden word and when an American information officer is forced under direct questioning to discuss it he calls it 'soft ordnance.' In the press releases and the answers to newsmen's questions, there is never any sense, not even implicit, of people being killed, homes being destroyed, thousand of refugees fleeing." [22]

Ordnance, it turned out, meant fragmentation bombs which exploded on impact and killed or mutilated all humans and animals within range of the sharp pieces of flying metal; napalm canisters, jellied gasoline bombs which exploded and sent out showers of fiery jelly, stuck to and burned into the victim's flesh.

Even the ordnance used to destroy vegetation during defoliation operations had to be concealed behind euphemisms, " 'Operation Ranch Hand,' " Paul Dickson tells us, "was the folksy name created in 1965 for a series of concentrated airborne chemical defoliation missions during which, according to officials at that time, the chemicals being dropped were likened to 'weed killers' — even though they could kill a plant fifteen miles from the point at which they were dropped. Terms like 'Ranch Hand,' 'weed killer' ('the same as you buy in the hardware store at home,' said on American official

,in 1966), 'routine improvement of visibility in jungle areas,' 'non-toxic,' and 'resources control' conspired to make defoliation and crop destruction sound like a major 4-H Club project." [23]

What of the victims of all this "pacification," "sanitizing," "defoliation," and "protective reactions?" While the weapons of war had to be euphemized, the people against whom they were used had to be dehumanized. Anthony Lewis wrote in the *New York Times* on June 12, 1972, that "some of those involved in the policy of heavy bombing and shelling must, unconsciously or otherwise, regard the Vietnamese as *untermenschen*, as creatures somehow not so human as us."

In his short essay "The Nonwhite War," Herbert Mitgang recounted a government official's reference to bombed civilian installations, and presumably the people inside those buildings, as "regrettable by-products." Mitgang, after referring to the withholding of bombing raid information from the American people, wrote:

"But the greatest omission of all concerns the nonwhite people on the receiving end of the terror falling from the skies. Watching Senator Kennedy's subcommittee on refugees attempt to extract the facts from Administration spokesmen is a despairing sight. A few days ago, in the old Senate Office Building, he asked: Why is it easy for you to tell us how many bridges have been destroyed in North Vietnam and the precise number of trucks hit along the Ho Chi Minh Trail but not how many hospitals, schools, churches and other civilian installations have been hit by our bombs? The evasive response by an Assistant Secretary of State was that these were not deliberate military targets but only 'regrettable by-products' of the violence of warfare."

If the "regrettable by-product" was the death of a South

Vietnamese civilian, the family of the victim was awarded thirty four dollars, officially referred to as "condolence awards." [24]

The "most shocking fact about war, Aldous Huxley reminds us, "is that its victims and its instruments are individual human beings, and that these individual human beings are condemned by the monstrous conventions of politics to murder or be murdered in quarrels not their own, to inflict upon the innocent and, innocent themselves of any crime against their enemies, to suffer cruelties of every kind. The language of strategy and politics is designed, as far as it is possible, to conceal this fact, to make it appear as though wars were not fought by individuals drilled to murder one another in cold blood and without provocation, but either by impersonal and therefore wholly nonmoral and impassible forces, or else by personified abstraction." [25]

The language and strategy of which Huxley spoke became an integral part of the Vietnam war in which politicians and military leaders distorted language to conceal and justify their inhumanity.

7

CONCLUSION

Once one has identified the language of oppression and determined that it is instrumental in subjugating individuals and groups, that the power of the word has been and is used to justify the inhumanities and atrocities of the past and present, then it becomes necessary to consider appropriate remedies. We can no longer afford simply to stand by and say "Oh, they're only words." " 'A mere matter of words,' we say contemptuously," Aldous Huxley asserted, "forgetting that words have power to mould men's thinking, to canalize their feeling, to direct their willing and acting. Conduct and character are largely determined by the nature of the words we currently use to discuss ourselves and the world around us." [1]

The implications of all this is that if we can minimize the use of the language of oppression we can reduce the degradation and subjugation of human beings. If the nature of our language is oppressive and deceptive then our character and conduct will be different from that which would ensue from humane and honest use of language.

One option to control the distorted, deceptive, and dehumanizing language is to prohibit by law the utterance of such speech. We already have statutes and court decisions prohibiting "fighting words," "obscene" and libelous language. On various occasions the courts have determined that such types of speech can be harmful to either individuals or society and hence do not warrant First Amendment protection.

In 1940 the Supreme Court said in *Cantwell v. Connecticut*

that "resort to epithets or personal abuse is not in any proper sense communication of information or opinion safeguarded by the Constitution, and its punishment as a criminal act would raise no question under that instrument." [2]

Two years later the Court elaborated in *Chaplinsky v. New Hampshire* the kinds of speech which could be prohibited: "There are certain well-defined and narrowly limited classes of speech, the prevention and punishment of which have never been thought to raise any constitutional problem. These included the lewd and obscene, the profane, the libelous, and the insulting or 'fighting words'. . .which by their very utterance inflict injury or tend to incite to an immediate breach of the peace. It has been well observed that such utterances are no essential part of any exposition of ideas, and are of such slight social value as a step to truth that any benefit that may be derived from them is clearly outweighed by the social interest in order and morality." [3]

The effects of language which denegrates and dehumanizes a group of people is no less damaging than the effects of "obscene" or libelous speech.

Attempts have been made through group libel laws to control the use of language which exposes citizens of any race, color, creed or religion "to contempt, derision, or obloquy." An Illinois statute which was upheld by the Supreme Court in 1952 (the statute was repealed in 1961) read: "It shall be unlawful for any person, firm or corporation to manufacture, sell or offer for sale, advertise or publish, present or exhibit in any public place in this state any lithograph, moving picture, play, drama, or sketch, which publication or exhibition portrays depravity, immorality, unchastity or lack of virtue of a class of citizens of any race, color, creed, or religion which said publication or exhibit exposes to contempt, derision, or obloquy or which produces breach of the peace or riots."

In *Beauharnais v. Illinois* the Supreme Court found against Beauharnais who had been convicted of unlawfully exhibiting "in public places lithographs, which publications portray depravity, criminality, unchastity or lack of virtue of citizens of Negro race and color and which exposes [sic] citizens of Illinois of the Negro race and color to contempt, derision, or obloquy. . . .' The lithograph complained of was a leaflet setting forth a petition calling on the Mayor and City Council of Chicago 'to halt the further encroachment, harassment and invasion of white people, their property, neighborhood and persons, by the Negro. . . .' Below was a call for 'One million self respecting white people in Chicago to unity. . . .' with the statement added that 'if persuasion and the need to prevent the white race from becoming mongrelized by the negro will not unite us, then the aggressions . . .rapes, robberies, knives, guns and marijuana of the Negro, surely will.' " [4]

In reviewing the history of racial conflicts and violence in Illinois, the Court stated that "in many of these outbreaks utterances of the character here in question, so the Illinois legislature could conclude, played a significant part." [5] Justice Frankfurter, speaking for the majority, concluded that "in the face of this history and its frequent obligato of extreme racial and religious propaganda, we would deny experience to say that the Illinois legislature was without reason in seeking ways to curb false or malicious defamation of racial and religious groups, made in public places and by means calculated to have a powerful emotional impact on those to whom it was presented." [6]

Four Justices dissented, including Hugo Black who warned: "This Act sets up a system of state censorship which is at war with the kind of free government envisioned by those who forced adoption of our Bill of Rights. The motives behind the state law may have been to do good. But the same can be said about most laws making opinions punishable as crimes. History indicates that urges to do good have led to the burning of books and even to the burning of 'witches.' " [7]

Justice Douglas also dissented, expressing some of the same concerns of Black and then warning of legislative encroachment on First Amendment rights:

"Today a white man stands convicted for protesting in unseemly language against our decisions invalidating restrictive convenants. Tomorrow a Negro will be hailed before a court for denouncing lynch law in heated terms. Farm laborers in the West who compete with field hands drifting up from Mexico; whites who feel the pressure of orientals; a minority which finds employment going to members of the dominant religious group — all of these are caught in the mesh of today's decision. Debate and argument even in the courtroom are not always calm and dispassionate. Emotions sway speakers and audiences alike. Intemperate speech is a distinctive characteristic of man. Hot heads blow off and release destructive energy in the process. They shout and rave, exaggerating weaknesses, magnifying error, viewing with alarm. So it has been from the beginning; and so it will be throughout time. The Framers of the Constitution knew human nature as well as we do. They too had lived in dangerous days; they too knew the suffocating influence of orthodoxy and standardized thought. They weighed the compulsions for restrained speech and thought against the abuses of liberty. They chose liberty. That should be our choice today no matter how distasteful to us the pamphlet of Beauharnais may be. It is true that this is only one decision which may later be distinguished or confined to narrow limits. But it represents a philosophy at war with the First Amendment — a constitutional interpretation which puts free speech under legislative thumb. It reflects an influence moving ever deeper into our society. It is notice to the legislatures that they have the power to control unpopular blocs. It is a warning to every minority that when the Constitution guarantees free speech it does not mean what it says." [8]

The effects of *Beauharnais* were minimal at best. James J. Brown and Carl L. Stern, referring to *Beauharnais* in their article dealing with group libel, wrote in 1964: "The hope that this long awaited legal ruling stirred in the hearts of defamation victims was vain. The decision produced no new similar legislation, nor has it produced increased litigation. In total effect, *Beauharnais* exists in a vacuum." [9]

In 1970 Prof. Thomas I. Emerson of the Yale Law School observed that "little remains of the doctrinal structure of *Beauharnais*." [10] It is his view that "our experience indicates that group libel laws are not the answer. In those States where they appear upon the statute books, they have rarely been used. The Illinois statute had, prior to *Beauharnais*, been before the courts only twice in the thirty years of its existence. Yet one cannot doubt that there had been countless violations." [11]

Group libel prohibitions would not only be difficult to square with our First Amendment rights, but would be almost impossible to define and circumscribe. Some of our significant and influential literature includes passages and language which deprecate or "defame" races, sexes, religious and ethnic groups. Shall *Mein Kampf* be banned from our bookstores and libraries? Shall the film *Birth of a Nation* be censored or possibly destroyed? Shall the dramatic pro-

duction of *The Merchant of Venice* be prohibited? Civil
libertarian John de J. Pemberton, Jr. concludes his questioning article "Can the Law Provide a Remedy for Race
Defamation in the United States?" with the answer: "Despite
the enormous risks inherent in uninhibited speech about
racial, ethnic and religious groups, the risks in suppressing
such speech are ultimately much greater."[12] The solution
to the problem of the language of oppression does not lie
in the legislatures or the courts.[13]

Hence, given the fact that we will always have with us
power-seekers and tyrants, some petty and others extremely
dangerous, who will use deceptive and inhumane language
to gain and sustain power, and given that legal prohibitions
are noxious to and futile in a free society, we have to turn
to other means for minimizing the uses and effects of dene-
grating verbal assaults.

There is considerable truth and applicability here to
Anselm Bellegarrigue's observation that "in the end there
are no tyrants, only slaves."[14] An oppressed group, or a
group in the process of being subjugated, has some power
to free itself from injustice and tyrannical rule. Those who
find themselves being defined into an "inferior" status have
the option to resist the efforts of others to gain linguistic
superiority over them. This usually is not an easy task
since the oppressor will not voluntarily relinquish the power
that comes from the ability to define others. But as Orwell
has indicated (see Introduction) decadent language has been
controlled by concerted efforts of minorities. The efforts by
blacks in the 1960s to define themselves was one important
strike against their white oppressors. Women during the
1970s have become freer human beings as a result of their
concerted efforts to eradicate oppressive language used for
so long to justify their second-class status.

Linguistic assaults often are used by persons who show no visible evil intent. While their motivations may not be to deprecate, the effects of what they say are damaging. Efforts must be made to make such people conscious that their speech is degrading to other human beings.

More difficult to reach are those who take the "What difference does it make?" attitude. They do not recognize that the negative labels we attach to people and groups have effects on their identities and perhaps their survival. Those with this attitude scoff at the need to stop calling women "chicks," "babes," "ladies," and "girls." These people see nothing wrong with labels like "colored folks," "boy," and "nigger." They cannot understand why "American Indians" resent being portrayed as savages, heathens, and barbarians. To simply point out the oppressive nature of their language to these individuals is not enough; they must be persuaded that such language is dangerous and has far-reaching implications involving inconsiderate treatment of fellow human beings.

These two groups — those who will discard their suppressive language if it is identified for them and those who will alter the language if persuaded of the viciousness of such speech — constitute a large part of the population. Their power to influence still others cannot be minimized, especially if their occupations place them in positions where they can institute a variety of sanctions on the uses of the language of oppression. Publishers, personnel managers, judges, teachers, students, librarians, educational administrators, and television producers should discourage the use of defamatory and dehumanizing language.

In 1971 the National Council of Teachers of English passed several resolutions regarding the need to define and isolate the language of distortion and oppression. One of the resolutions pointed to the need to detect "dishonest and inhumane uses of language and literature by advertisers." Another resolution urged teachers "to study the relation of language to public policy, to keep track of, publicize, and combat semantic distortion by public officials, candidates for office, political commentators, and all those who transmit through the media." [15]

In 1972 the Council established a Committee on Public Doublespeak which was charged "(1) to create a series of concrete classroom exercises (lesson plans, discussion outlines) which would focus students' attention on irresponsible uses of language; and (2) to alert the profession generally to the forces that in the committee's judgment are misusing language: government and its military, industry and its advertisers, educators, you and me." [16]

Leading publishing houses are now consciously trying to keep sexist and racist language out of their textbooks. The *New York Times* reported on September 12, 1974 that "a new, nonsexist era is dawning at McGraw-Hill, one of the world's largest publishing houses. In a sweeping assault on 'sexist assumptions,' the company will try to eliminate male-female stereotypes from its nonfiction publications — textbooks, reference works, trade journals, children's books and educational materials — to provide 'fair, accurate and balanced treatment of both sexes.' " [17]

The McGraw-Hill guidelines "prescribes highly specific changes in the description and characterization of women, and in the depiction of sexual roles. A list of forbidden phrases includes 'the fair sex,' 'the better half,' and 'the girls or the little women,' and lists such forms as 'suffragette,' 'usherette' and 'aviatrix.' 'Co-ed' should be changed to 'student' and 'sweet young thing' to 'young woman,' the guidelines say." [18]

In 1974 Lippincott's educational publishing division decided to revise its basic series of reading textbooks with
the intent to minimize the sexual and racial biases in school
curriculum materials. Lippincott editor Lozelle J. DeLuz
conceded that several stories in the series have included
ethnic slurs about the American Indian and have made him
"seem less civilized than the white man." [19]

Educators like Lillian Rosen at Public School 183 in New
York City began in 1974 to consciously eradicate from class-
room study the negative and dehumanizing stereotyping of
Indians.[20]

Officials in governmental agencies can take a lesson from
Casper Weinberger, Secretary of Health, Education and
Welfare, who in May 1974 ordered "that all references to
the sex of workers be deleted from employee rating forms.
One form by which the 139,000 department employees
are rated annually by their supervisors contains repeated
references to 'he,' 'his,' or 'himself' while making no references to females." [21]

To those who take the position that efforts to change the
images and status of human beings by altering language is
self-defeating and perhaps futile, McGraw-Hill Associate
Editor Timothy Yohn answers:

"The reality that concerns us lies in the perceptions of
the small children and young people who are ultimate re-
cipients of the material in many of our publications — their
perceptions and the values these instill. From a very early
age, children in this society are conditioned to accept the
role models arbitrarily assigned on the basis of gender. In
our opinion, this fact operates to prevent members of both
sexes, but particularly women, from realizing the full potential of their talents and their humanity. One aim of
the guidelines, but not the only one, is to alert our authors

and editors to the role of language in this inhibitory mechanism. An examination of our publications showed sexism to be widespread and deeply embedded in language." [22]

Such efforts will inevitably have positive effects on individuals who are persuaded that there is a viciousness in using the language of oppression. There are, however, some people who derive a psychological lift from using language which degrades others.

Little is achieved with this group by pointing out their use of verbal insults and inhumane language or the tragic effects of such speech. Their status in life is too interwoven and dependent on designating others as inferior; their failures in life and their anxieties demand scapegoats. Because of their insecurity, some men cannot give up the put downs "chick," "broad," or "girl." Some whites cannot linguistically treat blacks as equals; these whites psychologically need to express their resentments and suspicions for ego gratification. Hitler filled the disillusioned, anxiety ridden Germans with a sense of superiority by creating the Jew as "vermin" and "pestilence."

The empty lives of so many people unfortunately need to be supported with a sense of superiority which cannot be achieved through their accomplishments; hence the turn to verbal deprecation of others. The malaise of these people is an invitation to the agitator who can identify for them their imagined sources of trouble: the "mongrelizing Negroes," the "Jewish plague," the "barbaric drunken Indians." Having dehumanized these "enemies," the agitator then proceeds to suggest that all will be well if these sub-humans or non-humans are segregated or even eradicated.[23]

Supreme Court Justice Tom Clark, speaking of the language of group defamation, declared in 1964 that "we cannot expect the judicial process to control such utterances. Heads get too hot and evil too rampant. The *final* control must await the elimination of the three I's of this evil: Intolerance, Ignorance, and Ignobility. They *can* be destroyed. They are not the inevitable results of increased social intercourse. They are not inherited — they are acquired. They cannot be legislated or decreed into the hearts and minds of men. It is for us — in the words of George Washington — 'To bigotry, give no sanction.' " [24]

If "Intolerance, Ignorance, and Ignobility" are acquired then their destruction can partially be achieved by the eradication of the language of oppression since "the three I's" are not only reflected in our language but are aggravated by the learned language of deception and dehumanization. For those who wish to help achieve and live in a more linguistically humane world it is within their power to give no sanction to the language of bigotry.

REFERENCES

CHAPTER 1

1. Margaret Schlauch, *The Gift of Language* (New York: Dover, 1955), p. 13.
2. *Genesis* 2:19.   3. *Leviticus,* 19:12.
4. *Leviticus* 25:16.   5. *Isaiah* 66:11-12
6. William Saroyan, "Random Notes on the Names of People," *Names,* 1 (December 1953), p. 239.
7. Joyce Hertzler, *The Sociology of Language* (New York: Random House, 1965), p. 271.
8. Farhang Zabeeth, *What Is In A Name?* (The Hague: Martinus Nijhoff, 1968), p. 66.
9. Cited in Elsdom Smith, *Treasury of Name Lore* (New York: Harper and Row, 1967), p. vii.
10. R. P. Masani, *Folk Culture Reflected in Names* (Bombay: Popular Prakashan, 1966), p. 6.
11. James Frazer, *The Golden Bough* (New York: Macmillan, 1951), p. 284.
12. *Ibid.,* p. 302.
13. Jorgen Ruud, *Taboo: A Study of Malagasy Customs and Beliefs* (Oslo: Oslo University Press. 1960), p. 15.
14. Stokely Carmichael, speech delivered in Seattle, Washington, April 19, 1967.
15. George Steiner, *Language and Silence* (New York: Antheneum, 1970), p. 100.
16. *The New York Times,* October 21, 1969, p. 25.
17. Cited in John Carroll (ed.), *Language, Thought and Reality: Selected Writings of Benjamin Lee Whorf* (Cambridge, Mass.: The M.I.T. Press, 1956), p. 134.
18. George Orwell, "Politics and the English Language," in C. Muscatine and M. Griffith, *The Borzoi Reader,* 2nd ed. (New York: Alfred A. Knopf, 1971), p. 88.
19. *Ibid.*
20. Wilma Scott Heide, "Feminism: The sina qua non For A Just Society," *Vital Speeches,* 38 (1972), p. 402.

21. Peter Farb, "Indian Corn," *The New York Review*, 17 (December 16, 1971), p. 36.

CHAPTER II

1. George Mosse, *Nazi Culture* (New York: Grosset and Dunlap, 1966), p. xxxviii.
2. Grete de Francesco, *The Power of the Charlatan* (New Haven: Yale University Press, 1939), pp. 82-83.
3. Leo Lowenthal and Norbert Guterman, *Prophets of Deceit* (Palo Alto: Pacific Books, 1970), p. 6.
4. *Ibid.*, p. 7.
5. Adolf Hitler, *Hitler's Secret Conversations, 1941-1944*, trans. Norman Cameron and R. H. Stevens (New York: Farrar, Straus and Young, 1953), p. 184.
6. Adolf Hitler, *Mein Kampf*, trans. Ralph Manheim (Boston: Houghton Mifflin, 1943), p. 338.
7. Sigmund Freud, *Group Psychology and the Analysis of the Ego*, trans. James Strachey (New York: Bantam Books, 1960), p. 62.
8. George Devereaux, "Charismatic Leadership and Crisis," *Psychoanalysis and the Social Sciences* (New York: International Universities Press), IV, p. 154.
9. Kurt Ludecke, *I Knew Hitler* (New York: Charles Scribners, 1937), pp. 234-235.
10. Eugen Hadamovsky, *Propaganda und nationale Macht* (Oldenburg: G. Stalling, 1933), p. 16.
11. Alan Bullock, *Hitler: A Study in Tyranny* (New York: Harper and Row, 1964), p. 68.
12. Hitler, *Mein Kampf*, Preface.
13. Joseph Goebbels, *Signale der neuen Zeit* (Müchein: F. Eher, 1934), pp. 48-49.
14. Hitler, *Mein Kampf*, p. 475.   15. *Ibid.*, p. 106.
16. Ernst Cassirer, *The Myth of the State* (New Haven: Yale University Press, 1946), pp. 282-283.
17. Heinz Paechter, *Nazi-Deutsch* (New York: Frederick Ungar, 1944), p. 5.
18. Hadamovsky, pp. 11-12.   19. *Ibid.*

20. Richard Brunberger, *A Social History of the Third Reich* (London: Weidenfeld and Nicolson, 1971), p. 324.

21. Gustav LeBon, *The Crowd* (New York: Viking Press, 1960), p. 103.

22. Freud, p. 16.   23. Hitler, *Mein Kampf*, p. 562.

24. John Wilson, *Language and the Pursuit of Truth* (Cambridge, England: Cambridge University Press, 1956), p. 41.

25. *Ibid.*

26. Franz Six, *Die politische Propaganda der NSDAP im Kampf um die Macht* (Heidelberg: Druckerei Winter, 1936), pp. 18-19.

27. Hitler, *Mein Kampf*, pp. 118-119.

28. de Francesco, p. 125.   29. *Ibid.*

30. Adolf Hitler, *Hitler's Speeches*, trans. and ed. Norman Baynes (London: Oxford University Press 1942), p. 693.

31. *Ibid.*, p. 68.   32. *Ibid.*, p. 20.   33. *Ibid.*, p. 743.

34. The International Military Tribunal, *Trial of the Major War Criminals (Nuremberg*, 1947), III, pp. 522-523.

35. The International Military Tribunal, *Trial of the Major War Criminals (Nuremberg*, 1948), XXVIII, pp. 307-310.

36. Lowenthal and Guterman, p. 55.

37. *Ibid.*   38. *Ibid.*

39. Paul Tillich, *The Protestant Era*, trans. James L. Adams (Chicago: University of Chicago Press, 1948), p. 245.

40. See Erich Fromm, *Escape From Freedom* (New York: Avon Books, 1965).

41. Charles Odier, *Anxiety and Magic Thinking*, trans. Marie Louise Schoelly and Mary Jane Sherfey (New York: International Universities Press, 1956), pp. 58-60.

42. Hitler, *Hitler's Speeches*, p. 138.

43. Bronislaw Malinowsky, *Coral Gardens and Their Magic* (New York: American Book Company, 1935), II, p. 239.

44. Cassirer, p. 279.

45. *West Virginia State Board of Education v. Barnette*, 319 U.S. 624 (1943).

46. Grunberger, p. 330.   47. *Ibid.*, p. 466.

48. Earl Raab, *The Anatomy of Nazism* (New York: The Anti-Defamation League of B'nai B'rith, 1961), pp. 19-20.

CHAPTER 3

1. Gunnar Myrdal, *An American Dilemma* (New York: Harper & Row, 1944), p. lxxv.

2. "White House Conference on Whites," *Ebony,* 21 (July 1966), p. 86.

3. Cited in Ed Leimbacher, "Voices From the Ghetto," *Seattle Magazine,* (June 1968), p. 39.

4. Malcolm X, *The Autobiography of Malcolm X* (New York: Grove Press, 1964), p. 376.

5. Stokely Carmichael, "What We Want," *The New York Review,* 7 (September 22, 1966), p. 6.

6. John O. Killens, *Black Man's Burden* (New York: Trident Press, 1965), p. 50.

7. Winthrop Jordan, *White Over Black* (Baltimore: Penguin Books, 1969), p. 24.

8. *Ibid.,* p. 28.   9. *Ibid.,* pp. 32-33.

10. Lettie Austin, Lewis Fenderson, and Sophia Nelson (eds.), *The Black Man and the Promise of America* (Glenview, Illinois: Scott Foresman, 1970), p. 9.

11. Derrick Bell, Jr., *Race, Racism and American Law* (Boston: Little, Brown and Company, 1973), p. 2.

12. *Dred Scott v. Sanford,* 61 U. S. 1, 7, 8 (1857).

13. *Ibid.,* p. 29.

14. Irving Tragen, "Statutory Prohibitions Against Interracial Marriage," *California Law Review,* 32 (September 1944), p. 270.

15. "Intermarriage With Negroes — A Survey of State Statutes," *Yale Law Journal,* 36 (April 1927), pp. 862-863.

16. *Ibid.*

17. *Pace v. Alabama,* 106 U. S. 583, 585 (1882).

18. *Stevens v. United States,* 146 F.2d 120, 123 (1944).

19. *Ibid.,* p. 123.   20. *Ibid.*

21. *Naim v. Naim,* 27 S.E.2d 749, 756 (1955).

22. *Loving v. Virginia,* 388 U. S. 1, 3 (1966).

23. *Ibid.,* p. 11.   24. Cited in Bell, p. 88.

25. Stokely Carmichael, "Speech at Morgan State College," in Haig and Hamida Bosmajian, *The Rhetoric of the Civil Rights Movement* (New York: Random House, 1969), p. 114.

26. Lerone Bennett, Jr., "What's In A Name?" *Ebony*, 23 (November 1967), p. 46.

27. Martin Luther King, Jr., *Where Do We Go From Here: Chaos Or Community?* (Boston: Beacon Press, 1968), p. 41.

28. L. Eldridge Cleaver, "As Crinkly As Yours," *The Negro History Bulletin*, 30 (March 1962), p. 132.

29. *Ibid.*, p. 129.

30. Simon Podair, "Language and Prejudice Towards Negroes," *Phylon*, 17 (Fourth Quarter, 1956), p. 390.

31. *Ibid.*   32. *Seattle Times*, June 5, 1968.

33. T. O. Beidelman, "Swazi Royal Ritual," *Africa*, 36 (October 1966), p. 379.

34. *Ibid.*, p. 381.   35. Podair, p. 393.

36. John Howard Griffin, Speech delivered in Seattle, Washington, May 12, 1967.

37. Jack Olsen, "The Black Athlete," *Sports Illustrated*, 29 (July 8, 1968), p. 21.

38. Jack Olsen, "The Black Athlete," *Sports Illustrated*, 29 (July 15, 1968), p. 31.

39. Jack Olsen, "The Cruel Deception," *Sports Illustrated*, 29 (July 1, 1968), p. 15.

40. *Ibid.*, p. 20.   41. Cited in Bell, pp. 272-273.

42. John Howard Griffin, Speech delivered in Seattle, Washington, May 12, 1967.

43. Frantz Fanon, *Black Skin, White Masks* (New York: Grove Press, 1961), p. 31.

44. *Ibid.*, p. 32.

45. *Ibid.*, p. 35.

46. Myrdal, p. 29.

47. Fanon, p. 39.

48. Gordon Allport, *The Nature of Prejudice* (Garden City, New York: Anchor Books, 1958), p. 178.

49. *Ibid.*

50. Floyd McKissick, "Speech at the National Conference on Black Power," in Haig and Hamida Bosmajian, *The Rhetoric of the Civil Rights Movement* (New York: Random House, 1969), pp. 103-131.

CHAPTER 4

1. Cited in Jack Forbes (ed.), *The Indian in America's Past* (Englewood Cliffs, New Jersey: Prentice-Hall, 1964), p. 19.

2. *Ibid.*   3. *United States v. Lucero*, 1 N.M. 422 (1869).

4. Peter Farb, "Indian Corn," *New York Review*, 17 (December 16, 1971), p. 36.

5. Alvin M. Josephy, Jr., *The Indian Heritage of America* (New York: Bantam Books, 1969), p. 286.

6. Peter Farb, *Man's Rise To Civilization As Shown By the Indians of North America From Primeval Times To the Coming of the Industrial State* (New York: E. P. Dutton and Company, 1968) p. xx.

7. Josephy, p. 4.

8. Roy H. Pearce, *The Savages of America* (Baltimore: The Johns Hopkins Press, 1965), p. 21.

9. *Ibid.*, pp. 21-22.

10. Farb, *Man's Rise to Civilization*, p. 247.

11. Louis L. Knowles and Kenneth Prewitt, (eds.), *Institutional Racism in America* (Englewood Cliffs, New Jersey: Prentice-Hall, 1969), p. 7.

12. *Ibid.*

13. Arnold Toynbee, *A Study of History* (London: Oxford University Press, 1935), I, p. 152. For further discussion of the connotation of "natives," see Volume II of *A Study of History*, pp. 574-580.

14. Josephy, p. 107.   15. *Ibid.*, p. 108.

16. Farb, *Man's Rise to Civilization*, p. 253.

17. U. S., *Congressional Globe*, 29th Cong., 1st Sess., 1846, 15, p. 918.

18. U. S., *Congressional Globe*, 40th Cong., 1st Sess., 1867, 38, p. 684.

19. *Ibid.*   20. *Ibid.*, p. 685.   21. *Ibid.*, p. 686.

22. *Ibid.*, p. 712.   23. *Elk v. Wilkins*, 112 U. S. 94 (1884).

24. *Ibid.*, p. 102.   25. *Ibid.*, p. 109.

26. Estelle Reel, *Course of Study for the Indian Schools* (Washington, D. C.: Government Printing Office, 1901), p. 6.

27. *Ibid.*, p. 145.   28. *Ibid.*, p. 146.

29. *Ibid.*, p. 109.   30. *Ibid.*, p. 111.

31. Vine Deloria, Jr., *Custer Died for Your Sins: An Indian Manifesto* (New York: Avon Books, 1970), p. 10.

32. Vine Deloria, Jr. (ed.), *Of Utmost Good Faith* (San Francisco: Straight Arrow Books, 1971), p. 93.

33. *Ibid.*

34. *The Cherokee Nation v. The State of Georgia*, 30 U.S. 1, 16 (1831).

35. *Caldwell v. State of Alabama*, 1 Stew. & Potter (Ala.) 327, 335 (1832).

36. *Ibid.*, p. 333.   37. *Ibid.*, p. 334.

38. *Dred Scott v. Sanford*, 61 U. S. 1, 23 (1857).

39. *State v. Wise*, 72 N.W. 843, 844 (1897).

40. *Ibid.*, p. 844.

41. *In re Liquor Election in Beltrami County*, 163 N.W. 988 (1917).

42. *Ibid.*, p. 989.   43. *Ibid.*

44. *Ibid.*   45. *Ibid.*, p. 990.

46. *Davis v. Sitka School Board*, 3 Alaska 481, 484 (1908).

47. *Ibid.*, pp. 490-491.   48. *Ibid.*, p. 491.   49. *Ibid.*, p. 494.

50. *State v. Pass*, 121 P. 2d 882 (1942).

51. *Ibid.*, p. 884.

52. *Stevens v. United States*, 146 F.2d 120, 123 (1944).

53. *Porter v. Hall*, 271 P. 411 (1928).

54. *Ibid.*, p. 419.   55. *Ibid.*, p. 416.

56. *Harrison v. Laveen*, 196 P.2d 456 (1948).

57. *Ibid.*, p. 463.

58. *Allen v. Merrell*, 305 P. 2d 490 (1956).

59. *Ibid.*, p. 494.   60. *Ibid.*   61. *Ibid.*, p. 495.

62. Alvin M. Josephy, Jr., "Indians in History," *Atlantic Monthly*, 225 (June 1970), p. 68.

63. *Ibid.* p, .71.

64. Mary Gloyne Byler, "The Image of American Indians Projected By Non-Indian Writers," *Library Journal*, 99 (February 15, 1974), p. 549.

65. Edgar S. Cahn (ed.), *Our Brother's Keeper: The Indian in White America* (Washington, D. C.: New Community Press, 1969), p. 123.

CHAPTER 5

1. Deborah Rosenfelt and Florence Howe, "Language and Sexism A Note," *MLA Newsletter*, (December 1973), p. 5.

2. *Ibid.*, p. 6.

3. Jessica Murray, "Male Perspective in Language," *Women: A Journal of Liberation*, Volume III, No. 2, p. 50.

4. Aileen Hernandez, "The Preening of America," *Star-News* (Pasadena, Calif.), 1971 New Year's edition.

5. Emily Toth, "How Can A Woman MAN the Barricades? Or — Linguistic Sexism Up Against the Wall," *Women: A Journal of Liberation*, 2 (1970), p. 57.

6. *Ibid.*

7. Alma Graham, "The Making of a Nonsexist Dictionary," ETC., 31 (March 1974), p. 63.

8. Cited in Kate Miller and Casey Smith, "De-Sexing the English Language," *Ms.*, (Spring 1972), p. 7.

9. Virginia Kidd, "A Study of the Images Produced Through the Use of the Male Pronoun As the Generic," *Movements: Contemporary Rhetoric and Communication*, 1 (Fall 1971), p. 27.

10. *Ibid.*, p. 28.

11. Rosenfelt and Howe, p. 5.

12. *Aphra*, 2 (1970).

13. Joseph Fichter, "Holy Father Church," *Commonweal*, 92 (1970), p. 216.

14. Robin Lakoff, "Language and Woman's Place," *Language in Society*, II, p. 57.

15. *Ibid.*, pp. 58-59.   16. *Ibid.*, pp. 59-60.

17. *Ibid.*, p. 60.   18. *Ibid.*, p. 61.

19. Ralph Woods, "This Euphemistic Age," *Christian Century*, 78 (November 8, 1961), p. 1334.

20. Lakoff, p. 60.   21. Murray, p. 47.

22. Gordon Allport, *The Nature of Prejudice* (Garden City, New York: Anchor Books, 1958), p. 175.

23. Peter Jenkins, "H.H.H.: 'What this country needs is a nice man as President of the United States,' " *New York Times Magazine*, (May 28, 1972), pp. 22, 24.

24. Casey Miller and Kate Smith, "One Small Step for Genkind,"

New York Times Magazine, (April 16, 1972), p. 100.

25. Lakoff, p. 65.

26. Cited in Midge Kovacs, "Women: Correcting the Myths," *New York Times,* August 26, 1972, p. 25.

27. Judy Klemesrud, "Daniel Ellsberg's 'Closest Friend': His Wife, Patricia," *New York Times,* August 30, 1972, p. 24.

28. Miller and Smith, "One Small Step for Genkind," p. 36.

29. *Sail'er Inn, Inc. v. Kirby,* 95 Cal. Rptr. 329, 341 (1971).

30. *United States v. Yazell,* 334, F. 2d 454, 455 (1964).

31. *United States v. Yazell,* 382 U. S. 341 (1966).

32. *Randles v. Washington State Liquor Control Board,* 206 P.2d 1209, 1215 (1949).

33. *Adams v. Cronin,* 69 P. 590, 593 (1902).

34. *Ibid.,* p. 594.

35. *Mayor etc. of City of Hoboken v. Goodman,* 51 A. 1092, 1093 (1902).

36. *Commonwealth v. Price,* 94 S.W. 32, 34 (1906).

37. *Ibid.*

38. *Seidenberg v. McSorley's Old Ale House, Inc.,* 317 F. Supp., 593, 605, 606 ((1970).

39. *Sail'er Inn, Inc. v. Kirby,* 95 Cal. Rptr. 329, 341 (1971).

40. *Ibid.,* p. 342.

41. Leo Kanowitz, *Women and the Law* (Albuquerque: University of New Mexico Press, 1969), p. 176.

42. *Ibid.,* p. 177.

43. *California v. Cohen,* 81 Cal. Rptr. 503 (1969).

44. *Ibid.*

45. *Cohen v. California,* 403 U.S. 15, 25 (1971).

46. *Rosenfeld v. New Jersey,* 92, S. Ct. 2479, 2480 (1972).

47. *Ibid.,* p. 2484.

48. *State v. Hall,* 187 So. 2d 861, 863 (1966).

49. Elizabeth Cady Stanton, *et. al., History of American Suffrage* (Rochester, New York: Charles Mann, 1889), I, p. 854.

50. *Cong. Rec., 63rd Cong.,* 3d Sess. (1915), p. 1413.

51. *Bradwell v. Illinois,* 83 U. S. 130, 142 (1872).

52. *Ibid.,* p. 141.

53. *Hoyt v. Florida,* 368 U. S. 57 (1961).

54. *Ibid.*

55. Shulamith Firestone, *The Dialectic of Sex* (New York: Bantam Books, 1971), p. 88.

56. Julie Coryell, "What's In A Name?" *Women: A Journal of Liberation,* 2 (Winter 1971), p. 59.

57. *New York Times,* May 28, 1972, p. N38.

58. *Ibid.*

59. *New York Times,* September 13, 1972.

60. *New York Times,* September 30, 1971, p. 93.

61. Robin Lakoff, paper presented at University of Washington, March 15, 1972.

62. Kanowitz, p. 41.

63. Joyce Hertzler, *The Sociology of Language* (New York: Random House), 1965), p. 273.

64. Kanowitz, p. 46.

65. Faith Seidenberg, "The Submissive Majority: Modern Trends in the Law Concerning Women's Rights," *Cornell Law Review,* 55, (1970), p. 262.

66. Lakoff, "Language and Woman's Place," p. 61.

67. Diana Schulder, "Does the Law Oppress Women?" in Robin Morgan, (ed.), *Sisterhood Is Powerful* (New York: Vintage Press, 1970), pp. 156-157.

68. *Frontiero v. Richardson,* 93 S. Ct. 1764, 1770 (1973).

CHAPTER 6

1. Aldous Huxley, *The Olive Tree* (New York: Harper, 1937), pp. 85-86.

2. George Orwell, "Politics and the English Language," in C. Muscatine and M. Griffith, *The Borzoi Reader,* 2nd ed. (New York: Alfred A. Knopf, 1971). p. 87.

3. Robert F. Drinan, "The Rhetoric of Peace," *College Composition and Communication,* 23 (October 1972), p. 280.

4. Peter Farb, *Word Play* (New York: Alfred A. Knopf, 1974), p. 136.

5. See my "Foreign Policy and Demons," *Frontier,* 18 (December 1966), p. 13.

6. See my "The 'Nonmorality' of Cruelty and Killing," *Christian*

Century, 84 (August 23, 1967), p. 1065.

7. Cited in Edward and Onora Nell, "War Words," *College English,* 28 (May 1967), p. 605.

8. Paul Dickson, "The War of the Words," *The Progressive,* 36 (April 1972), p. 37.

9. Nell, p. 603.

10 George Steiner, *Language and Silence* (New York: Antheneum, 1970), p. 100.

11. *Ibid.*   12. *Ibid.,* p. 112.

13. Ronald Kriss, "Risk and 'Restraint' in Indochina," *Saturday Review,* 55 (May 27, 1972),   p. 30.

14. *Ibid.*

15. *New York Times,* June 16, 1972, p. 3.   16. *Ibid.*

17. *New York Times,* October 13, 1972, p. 12.

18. *Ibid.*   19. *Ibid.*   20. Huxley, p. 89.

21. "The 'Nonmorality' of Cruelty and Killing," p. 1066.

22. Sydney H. Schanberg, "The Saigon Follies, or, Trying to Head Them Off at Credibility Gap," *New York Times Magazine,* (November 12, 1972), p. 110.

23. Dickson, pp. 37-38.

24. Anthony Lewis, "The Cost of Phucloc," *New York Times,* June 12, 1972, p. 35.

25. Herbert Mitgang, "The Nonwhite War," *New York Times,* October 2, 1972, p. 35.

26. Huxley, pp. 86-87.

CHAPTER 7

1. Aldous Huxley, *Words and Their Meanings* (Los Angeles: The Ward Ritchie Press, 1940), p. 9.

2. *Cantwell v. Connecticut,* 310 U.S. 296, 310, 311 (1940).

3. *Chaplinsky v. New Hampshire,* 315 U.S. 568, 571 (1942).

4. *Beauharnais v. Illinois,* 343 U.S. 250, 252 (1952).

5. *Ibid.,* p. 259.   6. *Ibid.,* p. 261.

7. *Ibid.,* p. 274.   8. *Ibid.,* pp. 286-287.

9. James C. Brown and Carl L. Stern, "Group Defamation in the U.S.A.," *Cleveland-Marshall Law Review,* 13 (January 1964), p. 19.

10. Thomas I. Emerson, *The System of Freedom of Expression* (New York: Random House, 1970), p. 396.

11. *Ibid.*, p. 399.

12. John de J. Pemberton, Jr., "Can the Law Provide a Remedy for Race Defamation in the United States?" *New York Law Forum,* 14 (Spring 1968), p. 48.

13. However see David Fryer, "Group Defamation in England"; Manfred Zuleeg, "Group Defamation in West Germany"; Jean Peytel, "Group Defamation in France"; W. H. Bijleveld, "Group Defamation in the Netherlands" in *Cleveland-Marshall Law Review,* 13 (January 1964), pp. 33-94 for discussions of how group defamation laws have and are applied in other countries. See also Horace Kallen, " 'Group Libel' and Equal Liberty"; Anthony Dickey, "English Law and Race Defamation"; John de J. Pemberton, Jr., "Can the Law Provide a Remedy for Race Defamation in the United States?" Nathan Lerner, "International Definitions of Incitement to Racial Hatred," *New York Law Forum,* 14 (Spring 1968), pp. 1-59.

14. Cited in Mulford Q. Sibley (ed.), *The Quiet Battle* (Chicago: Quadrangle Books, 1963), p. 96.

15. "On Dishonest and Inhumane Uses of Language," and "On the Relation of Language to Public Policy," *College English,* 33 (April 1972), p. 828.

16. *Public Doublespeak Newsletter,* Spring 1974, p. 1.

17. Grace Glueck, "McGraw Hill Bars Sexism in Nonfiction," *New York Times,* September 12, 1974, p. 46.

18. *Ibid.*

19. Carole Martin, "Textbooks are Due for Change," *Seattle Post-Intelligencer,* February 20, 1974, p. B7.

20. Richard Flaste, "American Indians: Still a Stereotype to Many Children," *New York Times,* September 27, 1974, p. 46.

21. *New York Times,* May 8, 1974.

22. Timothy Yohn, "Sexism in Everyday Language," *Washington Post,* October 9, 1974.

23. See Leo Lowenthal and Norbert Guterman, *Prophets of Deceit* (Palo Alto, Calif.: Pacific Books, 1970).

24. Tom Clark, "The Problem of Group Defamation," *Cleveland-Marshall Law Review,* 13 (January 1964), p. 3.

The language of oppression has been of special concern to Haig Bosmajian (Ph.D., Stanford University) ever since the late 1950's when he began his research into the techniques of Nazi persuasion.

Some of Dr. Bosmajian's recent articles—notably "The Language of White Racism" (*College English*), "Speech and the First Amendment" (*Today's Speech*), and "The Language of Sexism" (ETC.)—have attracted considerable attention and have been widely reprinted. Adaptations of several of the articles appear in these pages by special permission.

Among the books edited or co-edited by the author are *The Principles and Practice of Freedom of Speech* (1971), *Dissent: Symbolic Behavior and Rhetorical Strategies* (1972), *This Great Argument: The Rights of Women* (1972), *The Rhetoric of the Civil Rights Movement* (1969), and *Obscenity and Freedom of Expression* (1974).

Books of Lasting Merit

THE CHALLENGES OF CHANGE Walter Cronkite
"An eminently readable, penetrating and moderate little book" (Library Journal) contaning a collection of outstanding speeches by the nation's leading news broadcaster. Includes a Foreword by Irving Dilliard. $3.75

MONEY IN POLITICS Herbert E. Alexander
A highly significant, fact-packed book about the role money plays in political campaigning. Foreword by Tom Wicker. $10.00

ONE LIFE—ONE PHYSICIAN Robert S. McCleery
An outstanding report prepared for Ralph Nader's Center For the Study of Responsive Law. Subtitled "An Inquiry Into the Medical Profession's Performance in Self-Regulation." $5.00

VIETNAM AND THE UNITED STATES Hans J. Morgenthau
A leading critic of American policies in Southeast Asia presents his views. Contains recent articles and new material. $2.00

THE POPULATION CRISIS J. Philip Wogaman, Editor
Much new light on fundamental issues is provided in thirty-four searching essays prepared by leading American ethicists, theologians, and population experts. Protestant, Catholic, and Jewish approaches point up significant areas of agreement and disagreement. $7.50

SEARCH FOR MEANING John U. Nef
An "Autobiography of a Nonconformist" by a leading American scholar with a great capacity for friendship and intellectual adventure. His wide-ranging reminiscences contain new insights about such men as T. S. Eliot, Marc Chagall, Jacques Maritain, and Artur Schnabel. $10.00

BRAZIL: AWAKENING GIANT Philip Raine
Based primarily on the author's first-hand knowledge, this authoritative but readable book tells how the Brazilian people live, how their political and economic systems operate, and why their nation has been beset by formidable problems. Introduction by Lincoln Gordon. $7.00

WHAT YOU DON'T KNOW CAN HURT YOU Lester Markel
Based upon the author's experience as a N. Y. Times editor, this timely book sheds considerable new light on how public opinion is influenced by the government and the news media. $7.50

SYMBOLS OF THE NATIONS A. Guy Hope
Profusely illustrated, this fascinating book provides for the first time up-to-date and accurate information about the historical origins and significance of the emblems, coats-of-arms, seals, and flags of 152 nations. $10

Public Affairs Press, 419 New Jersey Ave., Washington, D. C. 20003

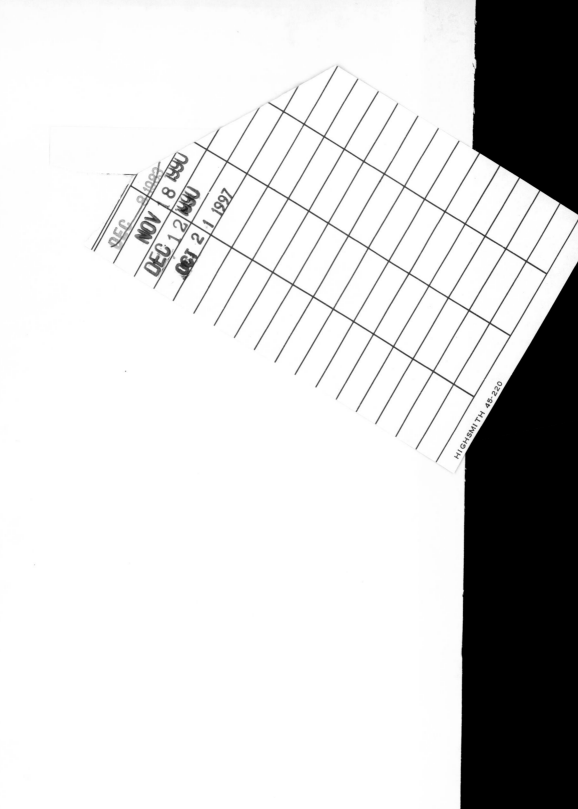